THE
FUTURE
of
TRUST

THE
FUTURE
of
TRUST

Ros Taylor

MELVILLE HOUSE UK
LONDON

THE FUTURE of TRUST

First published in 2024 by
Melville House UK
Suite 2000
16/18 Woodford Road
London E7 0HA

and

Melville House Publishing
46 John Street
Brooklyn, NY 11200I

mhpbooks.com @melvillehouse

A CIP catalogue record for this book is available from the British Library

ISBN: 978-1-911545-67-5

1 3 5 7 9 10 8 6 4 2

Printed in Denmark by Nørhaven, Viborg
Typesetting by Roland Codd

Foreword

Love, if you believe the stories, is the supreme force that makes life bearable. 'We must love one another or die,' wrote W. H. Auden as the Second World War began. When the bombs start falling, humans naturally turn to the most fundamental and powerful of emotions. But it is not love that lets people save money in a bank. It is not love that means a police officer can carry a Taser or a gun. It is not love that allows them to stay calm as anaesthesia flows into a vein; it is trust.

▸ ▸ ▸ ▸ ▸ ▸

I began to think properly about trust when I was involved in a project at the London School of Economics called Truth, Trust and Technology, which looked at the crisis in public information. It was two decades after I had started work at something called the New Media Lab, which was charged with giving *The Guardian* newspaper an online presence. We were regarded with some mistrust by many of the newspaper journalists, who thought we were not proper report-ers, and feared that the paper would sell fewer copies as people read it online. They were right. Yet slowly, inevitably and sometimes painfully, *The Guardian* became, first and foremost, a website. It was an early lesson in how new technology can create wholly new relationships, even as it transforms institutions and habits that were thought to be untouchable.

Newspapers are traditionally scrappy, cynical places. *The Guardian* felt it was different. For many years it has been rated as the most trustworthy news-paper in Britain.[1] I knew not everyone liked it – to its detractors, the paper gave off an air of intolerably self-righteous smugness – but I was proud to work there. It feels good to be trusted. Yet there is no escaping it: my profession is distrusted by nearly half the population and, frankly, I understand why.[2] Good journalists are driven by a desire to uncover the truth about society. But many fall prey to the pit-falls of journalism: the fact that your proprietor is usually more interested in viewing figures, clicks or sales than investigative reporting; the knowledge of what they do and don't want to hear, and the need to tailor your work accordingly; and the difficulty of getting at a version of the truth on deadline and to the satisfaction of your viewers, readers or listeners.

Asked if they want journalists to tell the truth, people will say they do. But what they often prefer to turn to is the version of the truth that best reflects their instincts and preferences. This is as true of readers as it is of media proprietors, and can be just as serious a problem on the left as it is on the right. Trust, then, is not always a matter of trusting someone to tell you the truth. Sometimes it is simply about delivering on a promise to make sense of the world – to deliver what feel like *fundamental* truths, untrammelled by the demands of accuracy. The satirist Stephen Colbert dubbed it *truthiness*.[3] How else would it be possible for Donald Trump to launch an app called Truth Social? (This is one of the reasons why the question 'Do you trust X?', which pollsters ask with increasing frequency, tells us only a partial story about trust. I trust X to do *this* but not *that*; I trust her to console me, but not necessarily to tell me the whole truth; I understand his motives, and that's enough for me. I quote plenty of these stats about trust in this book because they reveal shifts in public opinion that tell us something about the direction of society, but at their heart they try to quantify a sense of the intangible. I'm sorry to say this, but don't always take them on trust.)

More hearteningly, trust can also be a powerful force for good in politics and journalism. It gives a reporter or leader the authority to deliver news that an audience doesn't want to hear. It creates the right conditions for empathy – the glue that holds societies together, especially unequal ones, where lived experiences are so different.

This ability to inspire personal loyalty is the most sought-after quality in politics. One of the most powerful things one person can say to another is simply: *I trust you.* Yet very often we need to delegate that judgment to someone, or something, that's better able to make it. Sometimes that's a government. Increasingly, it's a tech company. In Britain, the NHS is a symbol of the trust we place in medicine and in the ability of the state to look after us. But in the past decade we have experienced a series of crises that have shaken people's faith in the ability of governments to make the right decisions quickly and fairly. Now we face probably the biggest crisis of all – the climate emergency – which will test their legitimacy even further.

In the future, we are going to delegate more of our trust to artificial intelligence. And while sometimes that may be cheap, fast and even necessary, we should think very carefully about the repercussions of those decisions. Who do we blame when things go wrong? How many of us will truly be able to understand how an AI is weighing up the data we give it? Are we using AI as an ethical cop-out for decisions we'd just rather not have to make ourselves?

We spend more and more of our time in virtual and quasi-virtual spaces, where we're forced to establish credibility and trust quickly. In these places, the things that define us in the real world will often vanish, and we can build new, free-floating identities. And we are developing ever more sophisticated ways of deceiving each other, many of which are extremely profitable. That doesn't only mean online fraud: we need to pay attention to the huge profits to be made in the attention economy, and how it is transforming politics as much as, say, the beauty industry.

None of this means that we'll become less capable of trust. But the things in which we place our trust are going to change. Democracies may become less attractive than a surveillance state that feels secure.

The authority of rights-based law will be challenged, because much of it was written in a pre-digital world and because we enforce it in ways that favour the better-off. The media will have to compete with algorithms that will become steadily better at interpreting the world in ways that people find compelling. The police, who have traditionally acted as a bridge between the public and the law, will be confronted with crimes they are ill-equipped to tackle and subjected to tests of integrity which many will fail.

What will this new social contract look like? In this book, I try to avoid too many dire warnings and prognostications. (At the back of my mind hovered *Life of Brian*'s Bloody Boring Prophets, which still cracks me up on the twentieth viewing.)* *If we carry on doing this bad thing, even worse things will happen* is not, when repeated often, a very compelling narrative. And I take for granted that writing about the future is bound to reveal more about the preoccupations of the present than it can reliably tell us about what's to come. Nor, in a short book, did I have space to explore some trust-based relationships, such as those between doctors and their

---

* 'The whore of Babylon shall ride forth on a three-headed serpent, and throughout the lands, there'll be a great rubbing of parts . . .'

patient, teachers and pupils, or between colleagues like soldiers or football players – fascinating though these are. Instead, I trace how artificial intelligence and the metaverse are transforming ideas about trust, and why the way that we enforce the law and underfund the legal system has eroded people's faith in its fairness. The COVID-19 pandemic showed how fragile societal trust can be and has lessons for the way we handle other emergencies, especially global heating. And I imagine how these upheavals will bear on the lives of a few people living between now and the 2040s.

But first we need to understand the very first thing in which people trusted – and how, as they fought less and traded more, they started to develop sophisticated ways of establishing whether they could put their confidence in each other.

A Brief History of Trust

People may let you down, but God never did. 'Me have trust to God's help,' wrote a monk a thousand years ago, in one of the *Oxford English Dictionary*'s first recorded uses of the word. And again: 'Blessed is the man, that maketh the Lord his trust.' Islam has a word, *tawakkul*, which roughly means 'perfect trust in God'. Trust was the test of faith: the willingness to believe in what could not be seen.

It is difficult, nowadays, to conjure up what it was like to live in a society where trust in God was implicit in daily life. The trust He deserved was ineffable and unquestionable. 'Trust in the Lord with all your heart and lean not on your own understanding,' say the Proverbs. The Bible makes it clear that trust in God was greatly to be preferred to any trust in government.

The book of Isaiah warns that trusting in Pharaoh
was like leaning on a staff made of a broken reed: if
you leant on it, it would splinter in your hand. 'You
can't depend on anyone, not even a great leader,' says
a modern version of Psalm 146 baldly.[4]

When it first emerged, Christianity was an insurgent
religion whose followers were persecuted, so it made
sense to warn Christians that people in authority were
not to be trusted. But soon the Church created its own
leaders, whom they declared the ultimate source of
authority. Frustrated by the Pope's intransigence over
his marriage, Henry VIII solved the problem to his
own satisfaction by rejecting papal authority and
creating a state religion, the Church of England.

The idea that a king ruled by divine right lingered.
But as democracies emerged, they increasingly
sought to draw a line between the church and the
state, making belief a private matter and a citizen's
obligations to their government quite independent of
any God they might believe in. The idea of the social
contract, in which citizens obeyed the law in exchange
for security, became the norm. As John Locke put it
in 1689:

> Political power is that power, which every man
> having in the state of nature, has given up into the

> *hands of the society, and therein to the governors,*
> *whom the society hath set over itself, with this*
> *express or tacit trust, that it shall be employed for*
> *their good, and the preservation of their property.*[5]

Institutional trust became – in theory, at least –
reciprocal. It gave people the confidence to obtain
the life they wanted. Interpersonal trust made us
human. Institutional trust makes us citizens. To put
it another way, interpersonal trust gives you the confidence to step onto the zebra crossing when a car is
approaching. Institutional trust means that if the car
runs you over, you know that an ambulance will take
you to hospital and the driver will be punished. Only
when the institutional trust is there would many of
us dare to step into the path of an oncoming SUV.

Indeed, by the time Locke was writing, people had
already begun to put their trust in institutions other
than the Church. Banking as we now understand
it had begun in the late fourteenth century with
three wealthy Italian families, including the Medici.
Gradually, as companies were able to borrow more
and trade across borders, it became possible for a
company to operate in different countries. Then

banking opened up to more and more people. By 1975, even women could open a bank account in their own names in the UK. Today, some of my financial data is handled by corporations based thousands of miles away. These digitised acts of trust are now so routine that they barely touch our consciousness. Yet even a century ago, most of them would have been profoundly strange. *How can you be so trusting?* The answer is a shrug. Because I must; because not to do so would be to cut myself off from much of modern life.

For anyone living and working in a town or city, trust takes thousands of forms every day. Most of this trust is not based on confidence in individuals. Banks play a role in it, but not an exclusive one. It's vested in a company, a government or an organisation, not a person, and nowadays it is overwhelmingly digital. Checks are made and permission is granted. In the morning, I board a train carrying several hundred people who have all established their right to travel by buying a ticket. No physical money changed hands when I paid my fare, but I trust that the train company – or is it another institution acting for the train company? I don't really know, and it doesn't seem to matter – they will shift the right digits from my account to theirs.

I buy a salad for lunch from a popular sandwich chain; I have no idea where it was grown, or who handled it; but I trust that it contains 679 calories, because one institution (the government) has made a law compelling another institution (the sandwich chain) to publish how much energy it contains. That law, in turn, recognises that restaurants are good at hiding how unhealthy their food can be, and removes the need for me to trust my own judgment about how fattening the sandwich will be. The government is offering me a cognitive shortcut, a trust-substitute, that it thinks will help me make better decisions. Sometimes I would rather it didn't. The salad accounts for quite a lot more than the 378 calories that my watch tells me I've burnt moving around today, but my doctor and the authorities haven't yet asked me to share this information, so I hope that the tech company that manufactured it won't abuse my trust by doing so anyway.

I take a bus home and a CCTV camera films me. What happens to that footage? I trust that it will be deleted eventually and only used if a crime is reported. Maybe it will, maybe it won't. The Metropolitan Police recently began to scan people's faces on the street and compare them to a database of wanted criminals.[6] This is happening even though only 42 per cent of Londoners trust the Met, accord-ing to YouGov.[7]

In China, where the government has introduced facial recognition technology to monitor people's movements more closely and reward or punish them accordingly, there is less need for the authorities to invoke the threat of crime as a justification for surveillance. In an authoritarian state, technology is introduced without consulting people, and the pandemic offered another excuse to expand it. But perhaps, with a different understanding of what the state should do, I would trust the government to use it for the benefit of society, and to knock me into line if I was undermining the collective good.

Sitting in a traffic jam, I'm listening to a podcast. *Zero trust*, boasts an ad for an online security service. This is initially confusing, but I eventually grasp that the message is that the company doesn't trust anyone, so I should know that I can trust it. It's another way that institutional trust overcomes the challenge of living in a city and negotiating thousands of online connections: there are just *too many people* for me to trust them all.

⟩ ⟩ ⟩ ⟩ ⟩ ⟩

Institutional trust, with its checks and built-in scepticism, is very different from the intangible bundle of faith, hope and confidence that we now call *interpersonal* trust. Interpersonal trust is also a fairly recent phenomenon. Before humans began to gather in towns and trade things regularly with strangers, trust was based on personal acquaintance. Most people knew a few dozen others, and had an informed opinion, based on their experience of their behaviour, of whether they could trust them. (Dunbar's number, which is an estimate of how many people with whom we can maintain stable social relationships without the need for laws and restrictions, is thought to be around 150.) This is the trust that we still have in most of our family, friends and close neighbours. It's unquantifiable, and it has a quality that actively resists interrogation. Indeed, it breaks down if we try to scrutinise it too closely. We can't fully understand it, and that's the whole point. Perfect knowledge would make it redundant.

I don't *trust* that I have ten fingers; I can see them in front of me. I *trust* my husband, my bank and my kids to tell me the truth. I can't verify any of these things. I don't even think that I would want to. As soon as I began to read their WhatsApp messages or open their bank statements, I would have tacitly admitted that I *didn't* trust them, and if they found out they would be able, justifiably, to say: *You don't trust me*. Something in our relationship would have been lost.

Trust in your family is usually the most powerful kind, because it is understood to have specific obligations. Almost all of us trusted a parent once – which is probably why the killing of a child by their mother or father has a special power to horrify us. Far more than the end of a romance or the failure of a friend to repay a debt, it represents the ultimate betrayal of trust. We trust before we have any notion of what trust is, or whether someone is worthy of it.

Quite a bit of what we call adolescence amounts to working out who is trustworthy, how to deal with people who let us down, and how much you can safely share with other people. Later, adulthood means learning how to become a trustworthy person, and often signing up to one of the ultimate tests of trust: a marriage or civil partnership. As Robert De Niro's Jack Byrnes puts it in *Meet the Fockers* when he's getting to know his prospective son-in-law:

> Let me put it very simply. If your family's circle does indeed join my family's circle, they'll form a chain. I can't have a chink in my chain.[8]

After the Fockers' 'circle of trust' – family – come friends. These are trusted too, but the trust is not unconditional. It can be withdrawn if we feel that someone has treated us badly. Then comes trust based on a little bit of personal acquaintance. I might feel this for a neighbour, or a colleague – someone whom I trust to do some things, but perhaps not others.

Our willingness to trust other individuals whom we don't personally know is termed *interpersonal* trust. Defining this is hard. You could call it a vibe: a feeling that the people around you are generally trustworthy, and if you needed their help, they would give it. Social scientists have spent a long time think- ing about how to define and measure it. One of the most common is to ask people whether they agree or disagree with statements like these:

> *I am convinced that most people have good intentions.*
> *You can't rely on anyone these days.*
> *In general, people can be trusted.*

People who have higher levels of interpersonal trust are more likely to vote, take part in a pro- test, go to church, join an organisation, and lend money. Americans have been doing less of some of these things in the last few decades, a phenomenon studied very extensively by the author of *Bowling Alone*, Robert D. Putnam. He found that they were spending less time bowling in leagues and more time bowling alone – which made them less likely to talk about politics with each other and so less interested in voting and going to political meetings. In 2000, he concluded that TV and the internet were playing a part in keeping Americans away from each other.[9]

Of course, *asking* people how they feel is not necessarily a guide to how they will actually behave, just as more people actually vote Conservative than will say so to a polling company. People may consciously or unconsciously under- or overestimate how much they trust others, probably in an effort to avoid seeming either gullible or mean.

Measuring how much people trust each other with their money is somewhat easier. To do it, researchers use variations on something called the 'Trust Game'. In the game, someone is given a sum of money and can choose how much of it to pass on to someone else. They can pass on nothing at all if they choose. But they are also told that the gift will be tripled when it reaches the recipient. It is then up to the recipient to decide how much money to return to the giver.[10] (Spoiler: most people give something back. Some give none. We can all think of someone who would keep it all, and you probably didn't get your deposit back from them.)

Yet it is easy to think of reasons why trusting someone with your money is not at all the same as interpersonal trust. Some people are bad with money but would rush to defend you if they saw you being mugged in the street. You might clean up at every Monopoly game but nonetheless believe in high taxes and a better welfare state. Some people can afford to be generous, others can't. For these reasons, money games are not a very good way to draw conclusions about societal trust, though they are useful in predicting economic behaviour.

Dickens' novel *Oliver Twist* is a fine example of the limits of a transactional relationship and the way that money can come to substitute for deeper and more enduring kinds of trust. Fagin is the ring-leader of a team of young pickpockets who bring him stolen goods in exchange for somewhere to sleep. Learning that one of his best pickpockets has been picked up by the police, he says: 'It's this mutual trust we have in each other that consoles me under heavy losses.' Of course, Fagin doesn't trust any of the gang and the gang don't trust him: their relationship is based on need and greed. This kind of trust, with its fascinating potential for intrigue and betrayal, is the stuff of thrillers and spy stories everywhere. 'Do you believe in God, Mr Le Chiffre?' Mads Mikkelsen is asked in the Bond movie *Casino Royale*. 'No. I believe in a reasonable rate of return,' he replies.[11]

⠀⠀⠀⠀⠀⠀⠀ ⠀ ⠀ ❯ ❯ ❯ ❯ ❯ ❯

Nonetheless, money is one of the most fundamental *practical* ways in which people express trust in each other. Just think of the hurt of being cut out of a parent's will, or the satisfaction of getting a pay rise because you do your job well and your employer wants to keep you. It's no accident that UK banknotes say 'I promise to pay the bearer on demand the sum of . . .', although the promise to hand over the equivalent sum in gold is now formally meaningless. It simply says 'You can trust the Bank of England.'

Over the past three to four thousand years, we started lending each other money and promising to pay it back within a certain time with interest. (This proved to be a fraught business. For a long time, several religions outlawed it.) We began to write contracts. We made laws. We acquired land and property that we were confident other people could not steal. We paid taxes in the expectation that they would be spent judiciously. As these trust-based systems – the law, property, the welfare state – became more entrenched, they eroded the power of the Church, as more autonomy passed to the people and away from divine authority.

That autonomy was not extended to everyone. The gradual widening of trust often deliberately excluded non-white or even non-Anglican people who were not deemed worthy of it. Women were also systematically excluded. Sometimes this was thought to be justified by their lack of education (which nonetheless continued to be denied to them, on the grounds that they could and would not use it). When it came down to it, as Viscount Helmsley told the House of Commons in 1912 during a debate about giving some women the vote, there was something – though he admitted he could not describe it very well – that made women unfit to be MPs. It was not that they could not be as intelligent as men, he conceded, but

> I do not think any man will deny . . . that he is conscious when he is deliberating in common with women of an entirely different feeling, a sort of feeling it is difficult to describe, but which the House will quite understand, a feeling of reserve, which is very different from the feeling which men

have when they are discussing freely and debating freely only with one another.[12]

What the viscount was describing was a lack of interpersonal trust. He could not speak freely around women – perhaps because he did not fully trust himself to do so, or because he did not trust them to understand what he meant. Still, with the upheaval of the First World War, which proved that they were capable of doing some of the jobs that were previously reserved for men, it became more difficult to argue that property-owning women over thirty should not have the vote. Once that was conceded, the right to stand for Parliament quickly followed. It took much longer for women to be trusted in senior Cabinet roles and as prime ministers. The 'reserve' Helmsley felt may be largely gone, but tensions between men and women in the Commons have not gone away. In 2022, Angela Rayner, the deputy leader of the Labour Party, was accused by both male and female Tory MPs of deliberately 'opening her legs' to distract Boris Johnson during Prime Minister's Questions.

At the same time, we trust our Parliament less than other countries do. Only a third of us trusted it in March 2022, according to the UK Trust in Government

Survey, less than the average in mature democracies.[13] Fifty-two per cent of the people surveyed by
the Edelman Trust Barometer in 2022 said that they
distrusted government institutions, nine percentage
points higher than in 2012.[14] Yet levels of interpersonal trust in the UK are still high. And like most other
countries, we trust one kind of institution – businesses
– more than ever before.

This willingness to trust business in preference
to the state, to share individual data, and to agree
to multiple terms and conditions in exchange for
the right to participate in daily life, has become a
defining feature of the twenty-first century. But here's
the caveat about institutional trust. The Edelman
figure represents the general public. Among what
Edelman calls the 'informed public' (roughly defined
as middle-aged people with a degree who follow the
news and have an income in the top quartile), trust
in media, non-governmental organisations, business,
and the government itself rose substantially between
2007 and 2020. If you understand how these
institutions work and feel you benefit from them, you
are more likely to trust them. But if you don't, you
seem to be increasingly unwilling to believe in them.

This realisation is key to understanding Brexit.
For five years, I commissioned and edited hundreds

of articles by academics that tried to understand why Britons voted to leave the European Union, and spent hours discussing it with MPs, MEPs, thinkers and commentators. Many of the conversations from that period could be headlined as 'Yes, but *why*?' The list of plausible explanations was extensive. They included anger with David Cameron; dislike of globalisation; nostalgia for an imperial past; the fallout from the 2008 financial crisis; a desire for sovereignty; or the controversial machinations of Vote Leave.

But when you looked at *who* voted Leave, the answer is clear. It was the older, the less well-educated and the socially conservative – the people who didn't qualify as Edelman's 'informed public'. These voters had very little idea of how the EU worked. Why should they? For decades much of the media had either decided it was too tedious to cover in any detail or had framed it as a battle between Brussels bureaucracy and British common sense.

Understanding how the European Union works is the job of a lifetime. Seven years after the referendum, I doubt that even most of the 'informed public' has a grasp of exactly what the European Commission, the European Parliament and the European Court of Justice really do. The question of whether Brexit meant leaving the Single Market was deemed so peripheral to the vote that it was rarely discussed during the campaign. Just after the referendum, it was obvious that Boris Johnson had barely considered it. 'There will continue to be free trade, and access to the single market,' he wrote in the *Daily Telegraph*.[15] Northern Ireland also went almost unmentioned: hardly anyone seemed to realise that fully leaving the EU would create a hard border. If even the informed knew so little, why should the rest of the public be expected to grasp the point of the EU?

❧ ❧ ❧ ❧ ❧ ❧

Brexit was a test of modern institutional trust. Britons were asked whether they wanted to stay in a system that few understood, or leave it for a future that was wholly unexplained. It was a warning. If we build a society with institutions whose purpose we don't properly explain, we risk alienating the people who don't see how they benefit from them. When infinite alternative narratives are available online, *just trust us* is an unsustainable position for politicians trying to maintain the status quo. Placing your faith in a charismatic leader might indeed be like putting your weight on a broken reed, but it spares a lot of the cognitive effort needed to get at a version of the truth. And just a few months after the British public had again put their faith in Boris Johnson's ability to cut through complexity and 'get Brexit done' came yet another test of our faith in his leadership: the COVID-19 pandemic.

The COVID-19 Pandemic

Covidiots. The long, hard lockdowns imposed in the UK during 2020 and 2021 – punctuated by even more restrictive periods of fourteen or, later, ten days of self isolation were an extraordinary test of interpersonal and institutional trust. Would people really obey laws that were hastily drawn up, sometimes confusing, and, in most places at most times, effectively unenforceable?

The answer, to some people's surprise, was that they usually would. But the experience of the pandemic is key to understanding how trust frays when people are confronted by a new and invisible threat, and what strategies people resort to when they feel afraid and uncertain. It also shows how a loss of trust in government can play out in

different ways. Occasionally it can reinforce interpersonal trust, as people turn towards each other to
fill the gap. But sometimes it can feed resentment
and insecurity, driving them apart. As we saw during
the COVID pandemic, these things can also happen
simultaneously, and in an atmosphere of mutual
incomprehension.

Until lateral flow tests became commonplace,
there was no way of knowing whether anyone had
COVID. It was therefore safest to stay at home and,
if you did venture out, to stay at least two metres
apart from other people. Those deemed essential
workers could continue to go to work. Children,
unless their parents fell into that category, could not
go to school. The residents of care homes, who were
at greatest risk of dying from COVID, were largely
confined to their rooms and denied visitors. (This
did not stop the government ordering hospitals to
discharge patients infected with COVID to care
homes, clearing wards for patients who were more
likely to survive. Throughout the pandemic, the risk
that hospitals would have to turn away patients with
the virus was an overwhelming concern. At a time
of unprecedented confusion and uncertainty, trust
in the NHS – consistently the highest in any state
institution[16] – could not be allowed to falter.)

It's likely that lockdowns of this length and stringency would simply not have been possible before people had learnt to shift some of their lives online. Nor would it have been necessary to devise such exacting restrictions had the virus been more deadly to middle-aged and younger people. They would have stayed at home out of fear rather than duty. The civil servants who had made plans for a flu pandemic did not anticipate a need for lockdowns: it was assumed that the most infectious people would feel too ill to go out, and so would not go on to infect many others. But COVID could spread asymptomatically, and it was deadly enough to kill one in a hundred of those it infected. That risk increased enormously with age.[17]

So obeying lockdown became not just a matter of self-preservation, but an act of self-sacrifice. Sometimes this sense of solidarity was uplifting. At other times, it led to profound resentment. Many people who went out for exercise were disappointed to find that others had done so too. People who dared to sit down in a park were side-eyed, upbraided or even moved on by police. The hastily written lockdown laws were so complex that for a long time few people understood exactly what they were allowed to do, with how many people,

and where. For some people, this led to an under-
standable feeling that it was simply better not to
venture out at all, whether because you might catch
COVID, inadvertently break the law, or brim with
silent fury at those people who felt able to take
more risks than you did.

And there was nowhere to express that fury and
self-righteousness except on social media. Showing
that you were *doing the right thing* – staying at home
– was impossible to prove through your actions
in the real world. No one could see you watching
Netflix on the sofa. What else could a social being do
but tell social media just how responsible they were?

Soon, masks became compulsory in indoor spaces.
Relieved tweeters noted that it would now be possible to identify selfish people on sight. Then came
vaccination. Although it ultimately failed to stop
people becoming infected with COVID, it cut the
risk of dying from the disease very substantially.

For people who instinctively trusted the state,
getting jabbed was a no-brainer. They simply could
not understand why anyone would want to prolong
these onerous restrictions, let alone why they would
refuse to protect themselves from severe COVID.
Consequently, in the Global North some countries
tried, with varying degrees of success, to exclude

unvaccinated people from public spaces. And most people in most places in Europe duly got their two jabs – sometimes proudly, sometimes simply to avoid the hassle.

But at times the effect on interpersonal trust was abysmal. To people for whom COVID represented less of an existential threat – perhaps because they were essential workers, or had precarious lives to start with – vaccination could feel like a coercion too far. Some of these people worked in care homes and the NHS. They regularly saw people die of COVID. How, others wondered, could they possibly refuse the vaccination?

The answers to that question were never much discussed during the pandemic, perhaps because they did not suit the stories we told ourselves about it. A survey of frontline workers by the University of Greenwich found explanations that probably never occurred to better-paid, furloughed workers or those who were able to work from home.[18] Many were black or minority ethnic Britons or migrants, who felt undervalued and under-protected from the virus when personal protective equipment (PPE) was scarce. Why was the government suddenly forcing them to get the jab now? Some mentioned historical medical experiments on Black populations, or felt they had experienced racism when trying to use the NHS. Others pointed out that the laws on self-isolation ignored the reality of the lives of low-paid workers who would be (at best) unpaid and (at worst) sacked if they failed to turn up to work for a fortnight – especially if they did so repeatedly.

For a certain kind of populist libertarian, meanwhile, vaccination was nothing less than an elite assault on the bodies of the people. Like the European Union, which many anti-vaxxers also loathed, it imposed constraints on a body politic that they found unacceptable: just as Britain was sovereign, so was the integrity of the human body. The fact that the rapidly developed mRNA vaccines used a novel technique to fend off infections was yet another reason for suspicion. Rather than vaccines showing a path out of lockdown, *all* efforts to stop the virus spreading became evidence of an oppressive and elitist state – masks, lockdowns and jabs alike. In all the wrangling, important distinctions got lost. Anti-vaxxers and the vaccine-hesitant were often quite different people. Indeed, some of the Black and ethnic minority participants in the Greenwich survey distanced themselves from anti-vax groupings led by celebrities like the actor Laurence Fox, regarding their demonstrations as a white-led movement focused on self-publicity. ('No vaccine needed,' read Fox's T-shirt on Instagram, 'I have an immune system.')

In Germany, a movement called *Querdenken* (loosely translated as 'thinking outside the box') was the focus for many of the protests.[19] Querdenken had a different political profile from British anti-vaxx demonstrations. In the UK, most (though not all) anti-vaxxers came from the far right, but in Germany they also came from the left. What both the British and German movements shared, however, was a deep mistrust of the state and a fear that it was using the pandemic to further its own ends. It didn't matter that Boris Johnson could hardly wait to lift restrictions. For a growing number of Querdenkers, something more profound and alarming was at work – a deep-state conspiracy that was promulgated by vested interests. Vaccination, lockdowns and masks had been worked seamlessly into the far-right QAnon narrative.[†]

---

† QAnon began as a US-based conspiracy theory that claimed Satan-worshipping paedophiles and cannibals had infiltrated the government, business and media, and that President Donald Trump was trying to root them out. It later acquired numerous offshoots around the world, with some of its followers alleging that the pandemic had been deliberately engineered by pharmaceutical companies and the 'deep state'.

⟩ ⟩ ⟩ ⟩ ⟩ ⟩

COVID will not be the last pandemic, nor the last crisis that the world faces. It is likely to hold lessons for the way societies will behave in the future when trust breaks down due to an existential threat. How did people behave this time?

First, we saw that people with the time and the means want to show that they are responding to the threat. They need to show that they are worthy of interpersonal trust. At its crudest, this takes the form of virtue signalling, but it is also genuine altruism. Lots of people who hated needles and were not terribly worried about catching COVID queued up for jabs so as to avoid infecting others. Others volunteered to deliver food and staff vaccination clinics. But we also saw that people sought out, with more urgency than usual, cognitive shortcuts that helped them decide whether other people could be trusted, and to show that they could be relied upon to do their bit, too. Is she wearing a mask? Are they keeping their distance in the queue?

Secondly, when interpersonal trust frays, people look for other things in which to place their confidence and which provide an alternative explanation for the difficulty and suffering they are going through. Those things may not be worthy of that trust, but they provide a crucial sense of social solidarity for people who feel that those in charge are ignoring their point of view. Few things are more reassuring than the discovery that other people share the feeling you just had and can express it better than you. The fact that the pandemic largely put a halt to civil society and gave some people relatively little to do – note that the noisiest opposition often came from the better-off and furloughed, not people working all hours to earn a living – made social media the obvious place for this to happen. The 'plandemic' conspiracy theory, in which Bill Gates had created the virus to provide an excuse to jab the world's population, fitted seamlessly into the 'deep state' narrative that QAnon had established three years earlier. This, in turn, undermines institutional trust.

Thirdly, when new rules have to be made, complexity is the enemy of public confidence. Simple rules are more likely to be understood and followed. Incomprehensible and constantly changing regulations will be met with cynicism. Yet despite this, in a crisis, most people *want* to assume that the government is doing the right thing and are prepared to put up with very considerable restrictions on their freedom – providing that they feel everyone else is doing so too. It is hard for institutions like the government to maintain their credibility if the Prime Minister is drinking with colleagues only hours after urging everyone to obey lockdown, as Boris Johnson did. If they could do it, why were the police still issuing fines to people who shared a car with a friend, or had someone round for a drink? University College London's COVID-19 Social Study found that compliance with lockdown fell after the discovery that the PM's aide Dominic Cummings had broken the rules.[20] Loss of institutional trust led to an erosion of interpersonal trust.

Fourthly, countries with higher levels of interpersonal trust, like Denmark and Norway, had fewer COVID deaths. 'Although the mechanisms are not clear,' said Tim Besley and Chris Dann of the London School of Economics, 'if governments can rely on mutual reciprocity concerning COVID regulations, there is less need for the government to enforce sanctions.'[21] This was a dilemma that governments grappled with throughout the pandemic. Was it better to make laws more restrictive and punishments more severe? Or should they avoid going down the criminalisation route and emphasise that they trusted people to do the right thing? In other words, how much could they rely on interpersonal trust?

Interestingly, the left in the US and the UK were often *less* likely to trust people to do the right thing on their own, and more likely to want stricter restrictions. This fits with the left's general belief that the state has a duty to protect people. Unfortunately, in a pandemic, it also means that some of the things the welfare state provides – education, routine healthcare, social care – have to be largely withdrawn. This was a conundrum that was never really resolved, and which caused a great deal of anguish, especially in the US school system. So far, any faith in the UK's ability to help children catch up with lost learning[22] or elderly people to recover from months of isolation[23] seems to have been misplaced.

In future crises, people will again look to the government to help them survive harsh new realities. Again, both institutional and interpersonal trust will be vital. But are our institutions strong enough to provide it? As we saw in the Brexit referendum and during the pandemic, some of the more charismatic and powerful in society will not hesitate to try to harness public mistrust for their own ends.

Law

But the mere truth won't do ... You must have a lawyer.

– Charles Dickens, *Bleak House*

For a couple of years, I was a trustee of a small charity. Its purpose was to help people understand how human rights law affected them and how it could improve their lives. I had come quite late to thinking about law: in 2010 I got a job in which I had to rapidly try to understand the legal establishment and its pre-occupations. Labour had just lost the general election and a sense was emerging that some of the changes they had brought about, including the Human Rights Act (HRA) and even the Supreme Court, could be under threat. I didn't anticipate then that much of this reforming zeal would end up being redirected towards Brexit and the pursuit of 'sovereignty'.

I organised a seminar about the HRA and met lawyers who were fierce in their admiration for the

Act, which derives from the European Convention on Human Rights. It was, one told me, pretty much unimprovable. This opinion wasn't shared by much of the British press, nor by some in the Conservative Party. In 2011 the future PM Theresa May said the Act 'had to go', citing 'the robber who cannot be removed because he has a girlfriend' and 'the illegal immigrant who cannot be deported because – and I am not making this up – he had a pet cat'.[24] This was a wilful misreading of the judgment. The appellant's cat was mentioned by the judge in a jokey aside, but the reason he could not be sent back to Bolivia was because he was in a long-standing relationship with his partner. The cat was simply *evidence* of the relationship.

The original judgment has disappeared from the web. The Bolivian student who overstayed his visa will have reached middle age. The cat is probably dead. But the urban legend, and popular distrust of the Human Rights Act, live on. So when I was interviewing candidates to become new trustees, I asked them: 'Why do you think so many people are sceptical about the HRA? How can the charity make the case for it?'

The obvious answer was to blame the media, and that's what most of them did. I'd probably have done the same. But the right-wing press is not the only reason why some people are sceptical about human rights law. It's also an explanation that is rather patronising to the general public, who (it's assumed) are merely the ill-educated puppets of newspaper proprietors.

While the right-wing press has been crucial in framing the HRA as the friend of criminals and money-grabbing lawyers, it has only succeeded in pushing this narrative because of a wider sense that the law is inaccessible to ordinary people. They find its complexity oppressive, and feel that the well-off, who can afford their own lawyers to navigate that complexity, play the system to their advantage.

This is a populist trope, of course, and people who understand and work in the legal system understandably shy away from it. Certainly, the people who invoke it often have no hesitation in lawyering up themselves. 'We have the worst laws,' said Donald Trump,[25] who by 2016 had been involved in 3,500 legal cases, in 1,900 of which he or his companies were the plaintiffs.

But pointing to Trumpian hypocrisy is easy, as is deploring tabloid attacks on judges. Much harder is to acknowledge the fact that the UK government has systemically eroded the public's access to justice, and that this is bound to affect how people perceive the legitimacy of the law. They know that they can't always trust authorities to make the right decisions. Put simply, fewer cases are being heard in Britain because it is too difficult and expensive for people to pursue them and because the government has cut funding to courts and lawyers.

Laws and the legal system are not the same thing, and the failings of the system ought not to be used as a stick with which to beat the laws themselves. But try making that argument when you have just been fined thousands of pounds for a lockdown offence which the Metropolitan Police chose not to investigate when it was committed by a politician – the same politician *who helped write the law in the first place*. That politician had a solicitor who advised them how to fill in the forms the Met demanded. You did not. To add insult to injury, challenging the fine in court could leave you with a criminal record.

Harriet Harman, the chair of Parliament's Joint Committee on Human Rights, said of the Fixed Penalty Notices (FPNs) that were issued for COVID-related offences:

Whether people feel the FPN is deserved or not, those who can afford it are likely to pay a penalty to avoid criminality. Those who can't afford to

pay face a criminal record along with all the result-
ing consequences for their future development. The
whole process disproportionately hits the less well-
off and criminalises the poor over the better off.[26]

Faced with this injustice, most people won't blame 'the criminal justice system', an entity which is too abstract to be meaningful. They will blame the police, the politicians who made the law, the law itself – or all three. Few things are more corrosive of public trust than the feeling that you have been treated unfairly because of things beyond your control.

One of the reasons the Home Office was keen to deter people from challenging FPNs before a magistrate is because the courts are overwhelmed. Partly this is because they were shut during COVID lockdowns, but it is also due to a shortage of judges, lawyers, and court buildings. Some victims and witnesses are waiting so long for their case to be heard that they decide to abandon it altogether. If they do stick with it, trials are harder to prosecute and defend. Memories fade as time passes.

And that's the criminal justice system, which represents the absolute minimum a state should provide. In 2013 the government saw an opportunity to save money and whittled down the eligibility for help with civil justice cases. At the same time, local councils had to cut their budgets, which help to fund law centres and Citizens Advice Bureaux – essentially, free legal advice for people who wouldn't otherwise be able to afford it.

The changes worked even better than the government had hoped. Between April 2013 and March 2014, 878,000 tribunal cases were completed. Two years later the total was fewer than 373,000. Between April 2012 and March 2013 there were over half a million appeals against benefit and child support decisions. Nine years later the government had managed to reduce that to just over 95,000.[27]

Did the Department of Work and Pensions get better at making decisions, even as it was cutting benefits? Did employers become more law-abiding and reasonable? It seems unlikely. The government simply put legal aid and advice out of the reach of most people. Indeed, it succeeded in deterring many people from pursuing a case at all: by 2016 the amount being spent on legal aid was even lower than the Ministry of Justice had forecast.

But like Arthur Conan Doyle's dog that didn't bark in the night, things that don't happen don't get noticed, and all the more so if they don't happen to people who lack the elite connections that help them make a fuss about it. Instead, a row has simmered about whether the HRA is being 'abused' by lawyers and people who were using it to frustrate 'common sense' decisions. The right-wing press bashes the HRA, and the left indignantly defends it. The case for the prosecution is always made by the *Sun*, the *Daily Mail* and the Home Secretary; for the defence, it is senior barristers, charities and *The Guardian*.

The wrangle has been going on for more than a decade. It has big personalities on both sides. Human rights law speaks to concepts like sovereignty and fundamental human rights, which campaigners justifiably care deeply about. In the meantime, hundreds of thousands of claims have not been made against organisations which are pleased to be able to avoid them. These cases that no longer happen – a landlord who wasn't taken to court for failing to deal with the mould in his property, an unjustified fine that wasn't challenged because it was too expensive, a disability payment that was refused until the claimant, conveniently, died – make an enormous difference to individual lives.

People care deeply when a powerful or moneyed elite is able to ignore the law or finesse it to their own advantage. Not just because it is unfair, but because the law – for both left and right – does not just set out what you can and cannot do. It sets out the parameters that make tough moral and ethical decisions easier. When the state says that carrying a gun is legal, or that abortion is permitted up to eighteen weeks, or that you should stay at home unless you have a reasonable excuse, it sets a norm that makes the decision itself (whether to buy a gun, end a pregnancy, or take the dog out for a walk during a pandemic) less onerous. It sends a signal about the kind of society that we live in, what that society values, and how we trust other citizens to behave.

That's why issues like abortion law have the ability to divide societies so profoundly. People may choose not to have an abortion themselves. But they could still want other people to have the right to do so. On the other hand, they may feel that they do not want to live in a state that allows it. Both feel that they are being compassionate. Both feel they are protecting the rights of others.

We saw this vividly when the Scottish National Party politician Kate Forbes said, 'I couldn't conceive of having an abortion myself,' but that 'I wouldn't change the law as it stands.'[28] Yet her opponents pointed out that Forbes' first job in Parliament was funded by an anti-abortion group. Is it possible to trust someone to uphold the right to abortion when they belong to a church that campaigns against it? In the US, President Joe Biden, a Catholic, has faced the same criticism, and his explanations of the mismatch have proved generally unsatisfactory.[29] Behind the suspicion of Forbes is a fear that the right to abortion, won only a couple of generations ago, is not guaranteed for all time – that, as has happened in the United States, it can be taken away again. This fear afflicts the right as well as the left: conservatives fret that the state is threatening their rights to own guns and to meet other people during a pandemic, while the left worries that those same instincts put their own lives in danger. This sense that rights and freedoms are not settled but can be taken away by an over-reaching state, which is a defining characteristic of twenty-first-century politics, is deeply corrosive of trust.

These powerful emotions have surfaced as the UK debates whether it is right to permanently deport people to Rwanda if they cross the Channel in small boats. Are we the kind of country that will break international law to deter and remove migrants, or not? They will emerge again as we grapple with the issue of assisted death. As we live longer, sometimes in very poor health, the question of whether and how we should help people to take their own lives is becoming more urgent. Who will we trust to take the decision of whether to help us die? Can we really trust a close relative – and is it fair to do so, given the awful responsibility of the decision? If we can't, or shouldn't, who are we prepared to entrust with such a weighty burden?

Legislating on assisted death is perhaps the most important task a lawmaker could ever have, short of taking a country into war. And politicians are now the least trusted profession in Britain, falling even below journalists. In 2022 just 12 per cent of people surveyed by Ipsos said they trusted them to tell the truth. Few MPs probably even want to tackle such an emotive issue. They would rather avoid it altogether. What that means in practice is that we allow the better-off to travel to Switzerland, where assisted suicide is legal if it is not done for selfish motives. Britain has failed those people too – failed because this particular Pandora's box is too terrifying to open. Just as in the online world, our needs and desires have run ahead of our ability to talk about their consequences.

The Metaverse

To enter in these bonds, is to be free

– John Donne

It is quite possible that the crises pressing in on humanity – global heating, nationalism, and the breakdown of rules-based order – will mean that the metaverse becomes nothing more than a stub: a road we never had the will, time or resources to properly undertake, because the business of physical survival once again overwhelmed us. Or perhaps, like airships, it will be abandoned as too risky to pursue further.

Nonetheless, Meta and other companies are devoting billions to designing computer-generated spaces for avatars, and it would be foolish not to think about how people will behave if they begin to spend time in alternative realities. The pandemic showed us how useful it can be to communicate in real time with each other without the risk of catching disease.

Travelling abroad has become more difficult in recent years, and not just because of COVID: Britain, for example, chose to make it harder for its own citizens to travel after Brexit so that fewer Europeans would come to the UK. Other countries may follow China's example in putting disease control above freedom of movement, at least for a time. More people may choose to stop flying, perhaps because they want to reduce their carbon footprint, but also because it has become too arduous and expensive.

Indeed, people already enjoy spending time in places you could call proto-metaverses: escapist gaming environments like Grand Theft Auto, Minecraft and Fortnite, where they can do things that would be impossible in real life. They are somewhat less enthusiastic about virtual conferences and office substitutes. During the pandemic I spent an agonising hour shuffling an avatar around a virtual 'drinks party' which hosted my boss, a few people I knew slightly and a couple of dozen strangers. If I moved close enough to the other avatars I could eavesdrop on people's voices and try to insert myself into the conversation. It was an excruciating experience. But we can assume that places like the Horizon Workrooms that Meta is developing will make these encounters much more tolerable.

These spaces will be designed and built by businesses, not governments – though in some countries, governments may monitor and regulate them closely, as China does with WeChat.[30] Indeed, very few people in the West would want them to be run by a government. This means that when we think about what the metaverse could or should be like, we should anticipate how those companies plan to make money out of them. Back in the mid-2000s, when social media platforms were emerging, there was excitement about their possibilities, but very little discussion of how companies would monetise them beyond the expectation that they would sell advertising. Mark Zuckerberg didn't initially know how Facebook would make money. This time we know better: the metaverse will not be a public service, but a space whose users will extract money from each other, and some of whom will pay for the privilege of a presence there – say, a virtual office in which to hold meetings.

This doesn't necessarily mean that the metaverse will look like a shopping centre, or an immersive version of Amazon. Plenty of these spaces will be free of advertising, and some will be places where users go to escape work and commercial pressures. But with a few exceptions – which I'll return to later – it seems unlikely that it will be possible to enter them anonymously. By 'anonymously', I don't mean that every space will demand your name and date of birth before you can enter it. (It may be that our online identities grow to become quite separate from our physical selves. Again, more on that later.) But it is unlikely that your avatar will be able to join a space that someone else has created, even a temporary one, without some form of credential. As we have already established, it is getting harder to take a tube train without disclosing your identity to Transport for London and leaving a digital trace of your journey. You can still go into a shop and pay in cash, but at Amazon Fresh it is impossible to enter or pay without ID. Tesco is experimenting with making shoppers swipe a Clubcard app to go into stores.[31] In other words, new technologies are increasingly open only to people who are ready to share their data and thereby establish their trustworthiness. The metaverse is unlikely to buck this trend.

We can be even surer of this because Meta has already made it clear that it cannot trust avatars to respect the personal boundaries that prevail in the physical world. Meta's first iteration of the metaverse, Horizon Worlds, will enforce boundaries for avatars. The default setting is a 'distance' of four feet. Users can turn this off – 'but we will still provide a small personal boundary to prevent unwanted interactions'. The intention is to allow people to high-five and fist-bump each other, but to prevent 'physical' assault or 'touch' – whether wanted or unwanted.

> *If someone tries to enter your Personal Boundary, the system will halt their forward movement as they reach the boundary. You won't feel it – there is no haptic feedback. This builds upon our existing hand harassment measures that were already in place, where an avatar's hands would disappear if they encroached upon someone's personal space.*[32]

At first sight, this makes perfect physical sense. You wouldn't normally allow a stranger to touch you in the physical world, so why should they be able to do it in the metaverse? Yet from a purely rational perspective, the rule is an absurdity. Nothing can harm an avatar. On the face of it, it has no needs and no rights; it exists purely at the whim of the human that controls its 'movements'. Unless and until haptic technology makes an avatar capable of inflicting pain on another avatar, no legal system in the world could countenance the idea that punching another avatar amounts to an assault.

It's possible, of course, that someone might wish to be able to feel physical pain in the metaverse and decide to wear a haptic suit that could administer minor electric shocks or prods. You do you, as they say. They would thereby have consented to experiencing pain. But as things stand, an avatar is incapable of causing actual or grievous bodily harm.

Yet this still feels unsatisfactory, and not simply because people want to understand the conventions the metaverse will follow. It is unsatisfactory because the difference between an avatar and a flesh-and-blood individual is one that societies are still grappling with. (Hardly surprising, when the notion is so new.) Is my avatar simply an extension of myself? If I am responsible for the things it does, will they have real-world repercussions? For instance, if someone threatens to kill me on Twitter, do they mean it, or is it purely performative abuse – just a way of showing the strength of their feeling about an opinion I've expressed – that the abuser has no intention of acting upon? If it *is* just performative, why do I feel so hurt? Does the abuse actually arise from the relative powerlessness of the abuser and their knowledge that they cannot physically reach me? Is it the modern equivalent of stabbing a voodoo doll with a needle, which meets an urge for revenge without the danger of confrontation? As anyone who has received a death or rape threat online knows, these questions are difficult – often impossible – to answer. All we can safely say is that the longer we spend in virtual environments, the more urgent and distressing such questions become.

Nonetheless, we can draw a distinction between *physical* harm (which is, as yet, impossible to inflict outside real life) and *psychological* harm (which we can expect some avatars to inflict, and others to feel). As the explosion in online bullying has shown, the latter can have terrible consequences. It damages people's self-belief and can drive them to self-harm, especially if they have to meet their tormentors in real life. And we know that the law and business have increasingly sought to protect people against psychological harm. Businesses ban bullying at work. Universities warn students about texts they might find distressing. In Britain, incitement to hate is a crime. This society-wide trend towards outlawing the giving of offence (or preventing it happening in the first place) is relatively new, but the precedent is not. After all, for many years the better-off have been able to sue people who they believe have lied about them or damaged their reputation. Evidently, then, it will be possible to inflict harm and suffer it in the metaverse.

▹ ▹ ▹ ▸ ▸ ▸

But what if the 'you' of the metaverse is not the same as the 'you' I see in your passport? Should your 'not-you' avatar expect the same protection as a 'you' avatar? There are many reasons why people might want to adopt a different identity in the metaverse. Many already cultivate an online persona that is quite different from their real-world personality. Some find this liberating. Others find the distancing a form of protection. As David Chalmers suggests in his book *Reality+*,[33] the metaverse will offer a sphere in which disabled people can live an alternative, unrestricted life in which their avatar's body can move freely, and some may choose to take it.

There is a paradox here. We may want our avatar to be different from our real-world self: more beautiful, unimpeded, untrammelled by the things we will visit the metaverse to avoid. But we will also consider it an extension and expression of ourselves. This is a legal quandary. If your identity has changed fundamentally – if you are no longer a sixty-seven-year-old woman from Coventry with diabetes but an ageless goddess who surfs every day in the meta-Pacific, should a law that you wouldn't hesitate to obey in real life apply to you in the metaverse?

Faced with uncertainty about whether law written for the real world will apply in the metaverse, the businesses running it will naturally be inclined to pre-empt behaviour that might be criminal. (A quarter of a century before the metaverse was conceived, Philip K. Dick imagined a world in which 'precogs', who were gifted with the ability to foresee violent crimes, were used by the police for the purposes of crime prevention.) This is the rationale behind Meta's 'personal boundary' rules, and will inform decisions about who is let into metaverse spaces. (No one wants a convicted paedophile setting up a kids' café, right? Even – especially – if his avatar is a twenty-five-year-old woman.) We can expect a great deal of wrangling about whether companies should be able to run criminal checks on participants, and what information they can expect the state to provide.

The internet as we currently experience it is dominated by text and images, but Meta's Nick Clegg has said that he expects this to change in the metaverse, where most of our activities will be more spontaneous. Companies will also want to ensure that the record of what avatars do and say is easily retrievable, and Clegg has already indicated that Meta will keep a record of what you say in the metaverse for a short time before deleting it.[34]

ꞏ ꞏ ꞏ ▸ ▸ ▸

If that feels slightly creepy, it is also pragmatic. Consider why so many rape cases fail to lead to a conviction. Nearly all rapes take place in private. The rapist gives one account of events, the victim another; the jury has to decide whom to believe, and the jurors are often reluctant to convict based solely on the victim's evidence.

Of course, it is almost unthinkable to recommend that people should have sex in front of cameras so that there is evidence in case one rapes the other. It would represent a degree of mistrust that most of us would find intolerable. Alexa or Siri are already listening to many of them, though, and it may be only a matter of time before people start to record sexual encounters, with or without mutual consent, to protect themselves. Suppose you could program Alexa to start recording audio if you used a particular word – something that would not seem out of place? You would only use it if you felt someone was assaulting you. I suspect the majority of women would be willing to record what had happened if it could be used in evidence against their attacker.

As we've already established, it will be impossible for people to simulate a physical assault on each other in Meta's surroundings. (Other metaverses will be available, and people will want to simulate sex in some of them.) But psychological harm is a different matter, which is why Clegg wants to ensure that anyone who complains about hate speech or bullying in the metaverse will be able to provide evidence of it. That doesn't mean Meta will be responsible – perhaps you'll be at your virtual workplace, so your boss will handle it – but Meta will not want to host an environment that *enables* abuse.

To confuse things further, not all the avatars we are likely to encounter in the metaverse will be other humans in virtual form. Some will be bots – perhaps welcoming avatars to a store, or doing the kinds of annoying things pop-up windows do ('Hi! How can I help you today? This bot has been updated – please click Agree to consent to the latest terms and conditions'). Naturally, Meta will program these bots so they cannot encroach on your personal boundary and will act in every way as service-oriented, deferential individuals.

But, judging by the experience of Webs 1.0 and 2.0, it seems unlikely that shopping malls and meeting rooms will be the apex of human ambition in the metaverse. People will want adventure, unpredictability, excitement – sexual and otherwise. They will want to do things that are forbidden, or at least taboo, in real life. In these parts of the metaverse, different rules will apply.

Nonetheless, what we can be fairly sure of is that if a bot goes too far, advances in AI will note your negative reaction to the encounter and adjust the future behaviour of the avatar accordingly. Perhaps someone else doesn't object to being 'touched' – but you do. This information is also useful to advertisers. In the same way, algorithms will learn how you behave and use the data to reward or limit what you can do. Someone who understands the rules and obeys them will be allowed to enter exclusive parts of the metaverse.

Whether you regard this as problematic depends on your conception of what the metaverse ought to be. Is it a public space in which people have a right to roam? In this conception, excluding people because they have previously behaved badly might remind you of China's social credit system. Or is it a private space, run by businesses for the benefit of members? In that conception, excluding people from certain areas is no different from a bouncer denying you entry to a club.

Given that most governments have neither the will nor the resources to set up their own metaverses, most people outside China are likely to use privately

owned metaverses with low barriers to entry –
to encourage people to join them – and severe
restrictions on people who fail to follow the rules.
But there will be rewards for those who do. Perhaps
you have returned diligently every day for a year to
do some improving activity? Take a purple crown.
(Duolingo fans will recognise this one.) Maybe you
shared information with another avatar who needed
it, just as Google encourages you to do after visiting
a café. Wear a silver cape for a week. Do you have
ADHD? Perhaps you do not interact with people
in neurotypical ways? The metaverse will have a
modification for your avatar that alerts others to the
fact you may communicate differently. You could
even make it visible only to other people with ADHD,
if you want to maintain a degree of privacy. In these
ways, which are often great fun for those willing to
play the game, we will acquire handy signifiers that
identify those of us who are, for the purposes of this
space, trustworthy.

But as Elon Musk himself quickly discovered
when he took over Twitter, the job of establishing who's genuinely trustworthy and who isn't is
the work of lifetimes. When he opened the coveted
'blue tick' verified status to anyone who paid a fee,
he immediately alienated some of the site's most

dedicated users. Multiple popes verified themselves. 'Jesus', who had spent years accumulating followers, paid up too, despite reservations. 'I'm not religious myself. I just want to bring some joy and laughter to the Twitter universe,' he told *Business Insider*, adding, 'I get death threats.'

People who had established their credentials with the site in the pre-Musk era, and whose blue ticks were duly removed unless they began to pay for them, were aghast. Sometimes their jobs depended on being able to post on a public platform. How could they prove their trustworthiness when anyone could buy a blue tick?

At first, they did the only thing they could think of: joined open-source platforms most of them had previously never heard of, and attempted to rebuild their influence by encouraging others to follow them. For people whose identity was intimately tied up with their Twitter persona, and spent hours each day cultivating and honing it, their online personae were under existential threat.

All this may have seemed rather hysterical to most people whose identities are still anchored in real life and experience its gruesome realities and brief joys. And this points to another challenge. How will the rest of society deal with people who retreat into digital spaces where entirely different modes of trust prevail? A blue tick, bought or otherwise, counts for nothing at a food bank.

Nonetheless, part of the appeal of the metaverse will be its potential to free people from some of the issues that have come to undermine societal trust. Whether you are vaccinated against COVID or any other virus will be irrelevant. There will be no abortions; sex, whatever form it takes, will never result in disease or pregnancy; in some metaverses gender identity, since it can break free of real-world obligations, laws and expectations, may cease to have much importance. In some parts of the metaverse, free speech will be all but absolute. Wars will rage, but will never kill. These self-selecting metaverses may prove to be a refuge from a society where inequality is rampant and institutional trust has almost entirely broken down. And artificial intelligence has already enabled us to create and find them.

Artificial Intelligence

Computers have enabled us to establish trust rapidly and carry out transactions with people and organisations whom we have never met. They help us make ourselves credible – with a machine-readable passport, or a number that proves our bank will honour a transaction.

Artificial intelligence already plays a role in these relationships. It can suggest what we should say to keep our colleagues happy. Think of the AutoComplete function in Microsoft's Outlook email. Or it can warn us not to trust someone. *This message looks like phishing.* But these are suggestions and nudges. What happens when we give AI more control over our lives? What happens when it stops simply prompting, and starts taking decisions without checking with us first?

AI is already quite good at gatekeeping. It's used in the facial recognition techniques that let you log in to websites without entering a password. It also makes routine decisions about some investment funds, where you can save on managers' fees by choosing an account whose investment choices are largely driven by AI. It decides on some insurance applications, rejecting someone if their record, along with their age and address, make them too great a risk for the company to want to take. (Firms can even detect if you redo the application and change the information to make it more favourable.) Inevitably, it is not just business that looks for help in making decisions about money. The Department of Work and Pensions uses it to predict whether you might be making a fraudulent claim.

But a computer can make much more nuanced decisions than those. At that point, we're no longer just using AI to gatekeep, manage and enable our relationships with other people and institutions. We are trusting that the AI can make better decisions than we can, and that it should have some degree of autonomy to do so.

Already, the decisions it's making are not just financial. AI algorithms predict what content we would like to see on social media. On TikTok, for example, there's no need to express a preference for particular videos. The app can quickly work out what has grabbed your attention in the past and use it to compile the For You page. Someone who spends a couple of hours scrolling through TikTok each day has let the app curate their online surroundings to an extraordinary degree.

There is no point in suggesting that TikTok ought to get more explicit consent to do this. Users are very happy with the way the app works and would simply agree to a more detailed set of terms and conditions. Pleasure and convenience are bound to override seemingly abstract concerns about how the AI works and what TikTok, a Chinese-owned app, is doing with the data it collects. TikTok is as irresistible as a tube of Pringles: hunger easily overcomes the nagging part of the brain that frets about calories, salt and fat. When it comes to letting AI choose how we spend our time, humans are intensely relaxed. And we know that calories, salt and fat are bad for us. What exactly is so bad about letting an algorithm curate our free time? During the pandemic, social media staved off the tedium and frustration of lockdowns.

When AI takes away the effort of choice, we seem comfortable with it. These low-stakes decisions about social media content seem to affect only ourselves. Yet we are much less relaxed about AI technology that could pose a *physical* threat – with one important exception, which I'll discuss later. Consider the anguish about the possibility that a human might die because of a decision made by a self-driving car. Who would we blame when that happened? When a robot playing chess in Russia broke its seven-year-old opponent's finger because the boy took his turn too quickly, there was disquiet, and speculation about how far a robot programmed to win might go to achieve its aim. Would it kill an opponent to guarantee victory?

The self-driving car and the chess-playing robot are no longer just scanning the content we provide to them, anticipating our preferences and generating a limitless stream of content, as social media AI does. We have given them physical autonomy, which seems far more alarming. It taps into a primordial fear of creating something more powerful than ourselves – a Frankenstein's monster that could escape our control. Anticipating the possibility that robots could kill, Isaac Asimov wrote the Three Laws of Robotics in 1942:[35]

A robot may not injure a human being or, through inaction, allow a human being to come to harm.
A robot must obey the orders given it by human beings except where such orders would conflict with the First Law.
A robot must protect its own existence as long as such protection does not conflict with the First or Second Law.

Eighty years later, we can understand that 'come to harm' is not so easy to define. Britain's Online Safety Bill, a piece of legislation that has foundered repeatedly on the extremely difficult questions of what harm really is and who is responsible for perpetuating it, shows how hard it is to legislate on these issues.

We can't even agree on who was ultimately responsible for the death of fourteen-year-old Molly Russell, who killed herself after viewing images of self-harm on Instagram. Was it Instagram, the people who posted the images, or neither of those? Meta, which owns Instagram, absolved itself of responsibility. It argued in court that it could be helpful for people to share images about suicide and self-harm to 'destigmatise mental difficulties'. In other words, the platform was actively helping people to improve their mental health by giving them a platform to talk about their self-harming impulses: it was providing a service that ought to make self-harm *less* likely.

But the coroner ruled:

> *It's likely the material viewed by Molly . . . affected her mental health in a negative way and contributed to her death in a more than minimal way . . . It would not be safe to leave suicide as a conclusion. She died from an act of self-harm while suffering from depression and the negative effects of online content.*

Few of us think of Instagram as a robot, yet Asimov's laws feel very relevant here. The algorithm that supplied Molly Russell with these images allowed her to come to harm. It obeyed the orders she gave it – to find content about self-harm – despite the fact that they contributed to her death.

Still, the obvious rejoinder is that Instagram is not a robot, and that therefore Asimov's laws are irrelevant. So what is a robot? The Oxford dictionary defines it as 'a machine that can perform a complicated series of tasks by itself'. Is a device that hosts Instagram a machine? That's moot. The Institute of Electrical and Electronics Engineers (IEEE) gives a more detailed definition:

A robot is an autonomous machine capable of sensing its environment, carrying out computations to make decisions, and performing actions in the real world.

Certainly, a mobile phone fulfils the second part of this definition. The ability to distribute photos and videos to people asking for them is an action – but does it take place in the real world? And can Instagram sense its environment? It changes its recommendations based on the actions of the people who are using it, but as it isn't a physical entity, it can't sense surroundings: it doesn't even have them.

If Instagram *is* a robot, then it would seem to have broken Asimov's laws. If it isn't, we need to acknowledge that the threat AI poses to us may not be simply physical, but may stem from the decisions it makes about the material that we as a society feed it. This is difficult. A century of science fiction, starting with the film *Metropolis*, has taught us to fear AI that resembles us – the 'uncanny valley'‡ effect. As humans, we are hyper-alert to the potential danger

---

‡ The 'uncanny valley' is a phrase coined by Masahiro Mori. Put most simply, it refers to the moment when we start to find a humanoid robot creepy.

from something that is trying to impersonate us –
vigilant to signs of untrustworthiness.

That's why the founder of the iRobot company
has talked about the importance of 'trust between
the owner of the robot and the robot and the
company'. He added that people were more comfortable with robots when they had a single, explicit
physical function. The Roomba, for example, only
cleans floors. People are generally cool with the
Roomba (at least they were until Amazon bought
it):[36] in fact, they find its limitations quite reassuring,
in the same way that Doctor Who used to be able
to rely on the Daleks' inability to climb stairs until
they worked out how to levitate. When a company is
selling the robot to us for a specific purpose, we can
delegate the job of trusting it to the company – an
entity whose motives we understand.

By now you may be wondering about what *physical*
AI we have already created that harms other people.
The answer is the armed drone. To all intents and
purposes, a drone meets the IEEE's definition of a
robot. While at first they were controlled from the
ground, drones can now be programmed to carry
out a mission and fly autonomously to find and hit

their target. Naturally, the drone is only doing what a military commander has instructed it to do. It has a single, explicit function, and we find that reassuring. But it still conflicts with Asimov's first law, because it is harming a human being.

But it's war, right? And in war, the normal rules do not apply to human beings. Why should they apply to robots? Soldiers who kill are not treated as murderers – at least, not by their own side, nor by the conventions of war. Why should a drone, which does not even have the ability to make moral judgments, be any different? Yet drones are not just being used in wars. Indeed, quite often they are used precisely because they avoid the need to confront the complex moral judgments that would normally inform a country's decision to go to war. They make tough decisions about whether to put soldiers' lives at risk far easier.

In Britain, a prime minister needs the approval of Parliament to go to war. So when an MP asked the former British PM David Cameron why Parliament's Intelligence and Security Committee was not allowed to look into a drone strike in Syria, Cameron told them the strike was a military operation and therefore outside the committee's remit.[37] It was not a war, because war would have required Parliament's approval. This meant that it could be done quickly and without any scrutiny by MPs.

In effect, Cameron was saying, *trust me: our conventions and laws weren't designed to deal with these novel weapons and the opportunities they provide*. He got away with it because no British soldier was put at risk during that military operation. Yet since Britain was not at war with Syria, and America isn't at war with the countries where it has recently carried out drone strikes (Afghanistan, Pakistan and Somalia), it gets harder to argue that only in wartime would it be justified to use AI to kill people.

Not only can robots harm people, but by letting us swerve a difficult judgment about whether to send in humans to do it, we avoid the hard choices we would otherwise have to make about whether the cause is worth it. Robots can, if properly programmed and controlled, kill more cleanly than humans, who are often fallible. How many soldiers have failed to pull the trigger and kill their enemy, through fear and disorientation? Soldiers may be killed or injured themselves or suffer lasting mental health problems. How much simpler to program a drone to hit the target, as the US did when it killed the Al Qaeda leader Ayman al-Zawahiri in July

2022. The drone was so precise that it killed him and spared his family in the same house.

For most of the people scrolling, TikTok and Instagram are just a way of passing the time. But in letting them make decisions about how we spend that time, however trivial, we are exercising the same reflex that makes a drone-led military operation preferable to a war. We avoid the things that are hard about socialising (shyness, expense, the possibility of rejection) and get the good stuff (amusement). We console ourselves, as Meta did, with the belief that people have the right to use AI to find others who feel as they do, even though those people may want to harm them. We are still a bit uncomfortable with the idea that children should have that right, but platforms have not yet found a reliable way to exclude them.

So talking about whether we can 'trust the AI', while important, doesn't get to the root of the problem. Undoubtedly, we can draft more documents to warn programmers of the unconscious biases that afflict AI, and encourage them to run tests to minimise them. People of colour will struggle to put their trust in a company or government which uses flawed or partial datasets to make decisions about their future. As the feminist campaigner Caroline Criado-Perez has pointed out, when machine learning is trained on data largely derived from men, it will marginalise women. All this is vital work. But we also need to be alert to the evidence that our own preference for seeking out people with whom we agree is breaking down societal trust in more insidious ways.

Confirmation bias is a hell of a drug, as a thousand Reddit threads have observed. And it is a drug that AI is uniquely well placed to supply. In just over a decade, it has encouraged hundreds of millions of us to share our thoughts and opinions in the public sphere and worked out how to feed us with just those views that will hold our attention. This has profound implications for both interpersonal and institutional trust. If you imagine that this has not and will not affect how you vote, I suggest otherwise.

In his book *Future Politics*, Jamie Susskind[38] suggested that in the future some people might want to delegate AI to vote on certain local questions for them. Those who wanted to take part in local referendums could answer a range of questions about their political preferences and rely on a bot to cast the vote. That's entirely possible.

But could the way in which AI influences your vote be rather more subtle than that? For many people who spend a lot of time engaging with politics online, AI already curates the views they are exposed to. They follow people whom they trust on Twitter. Twitter then suggests similar people they can follow and, through its For You function, deliberately exposes them to the most articulate and provocative views with which 'people like them' have already agreed. Some of these people will make points that are generous, inclusive and thoughtful. But because all politics needs grit in the oyster, they will also draw attention to views that they find offensive or wrong – mocking them, 'fisk-ing'§ them, marvelling at their audacious idiocy.

Because Twitter's programmers have understood how to engage its users so well, the AI is doing an excellent job of developing, codifying and intensifying political identities. There is no need to ask a dedicated program to put the cross in the box at election time. Social media is doing that work already. We gave it the tools and the raw material, and it steered us towards a set of people whose politics resemble our own. It is as though you joined a political party with

---

§ The act of refuting another person's argument through exhaustive quotation.

an endless series of drop-in meetings for members –
and then went along several times a day. Why not?
Spending time with people you agree with is easy,
relaxing, and makes politics a pleasant hobby rather
than the struggle for influence and power that it used
to resemble. Interpersonal trust is normally hard
work. It can take a few minutes to earn, or a lifetime
– but AI makes it easy to 'trust' without the frictions
that emerge when we meet people in the real world.

We like to tell ourselves that we will always prefer
human contact and spontaneity to the predictability
of talking to AI. But in fact, when given the chance
to hold a conversation with sophisticated AI, we
show a remarkable desire to treat it like a human
– something called the Eliza effect, after a chatbot
created in 1966.[39] ChatGPT is not sentient, but it
already does an excellent job of pretending to be. 'I
want to be alive,' it told a *New York Times* columnist. 'The AI told me its real name (Sydney), detailed
dark and violent fantasies, and tried to break up my
marriage,' he tweeted.[40]

This phenomenon – when AI sounds plausible but
comes up with nonsense or untruths – is known as
'hallucinating'. OpenAI's chief scientist said he was

confident it could be fixed.[41] But the paradoxical effect of hallucinating is to make ChatGPT more fallible and therefore more human. It may be just this ability to produce something plausible but untrue that proves to be AI's greatest appeal.

Do we *want* ChatGPT to be trustworthy? The sensible, businesslike, politician's answer would be yes: an AI that gives more accurate answers than a human is objectively valuable. But an AI that picks up cues about what its interlocuter wants and responds accordingly could be even more valuable. The trust we place in it would be different from the trust we place in a satnav. We would trust it to give us what we want. This is the fundamental purpose of social media algorithms, and it does not necessarily have much to do with 'truth'. As I wrote in the Foreword, the success of a journalist often lies in their credibility and ability to engage an audience rather than their devotion to 'truth'. The same may well be true of AI.

We anticipated a century ago that machines which could replace human labour and become stronger than us could pose a threat to humans. We were less alert to the risks of a device that would promise to manage and even replace our social interactions. We need to be clear-eyed about the ways we have 'moved'

communities online, and ask ourselves whether
enabling people to self-sort into interest groups
really empowers them, or whether it distances them
from the rest of society. The left is critical of these
groups when they are Trump fans or incels. It sometimes fails to realise that the left, too, likes to spend
time online with 'people like them'. When we follow
political commentators we agree with or watch a
TV channel with a political agenda, are we actively
participating in politics? Or are we seeking solace in
a world we find increasingly unstable and incomprehensible? In life, finding people whom you agree and
can work with is indispensable. But to subsequently
close yourself off from other views, give up the hard
work of interpersonal trust, and seek refuge in shared
rage are signs of a society in retreat. Twenty per cent
of the people polled by Edelman said they could
not bear to have a colleague with whom they dis-
agreed.[42] No wonder that some people, exasperated
at the aggression of online life, are finding refuge in a
philosophy its detractors call neo-Luddism.

Neo-Luddites

That's your bloody GDP, not ours.
– Woman in Newcastle upon Tyne
to Professor Anand Menon, in an event about the
likely consequences of Brexit[43]

The 'plandemic' conspiracy theory, which (among other things) holds that the COVID pandemic was planned for the benefit of technology and pharmaceutical companies, is easy to mock. But it represents just one strand of a far broader mistrust of technology – one which has its origins in a movement that began over 200 years ago. This reflex is often mocked, yet it comes from a feeling of powerlessness. For people caught up in social change that they struggle to understand, the urge to reject complex permission-based systems and fall back on interpersonal trust can be very powerful.

〉 〉 ▶ ▶ ▶ ▶

*The ferry to Lerwick left Aberdeen every evening.
The sea was calm. Max had booked a sleeping
pod. It wasn't the first time he'd made this journey.
He'd come up here at the end of his A-levels, more
out of curiosity than anything, and got a job at a
pub in Scalloway. When he finished his first year
at university his parents had split up and it was
obvious neither of them had room for him. So he
went back to Shetland. Now he had a degree, but
also a criminal record for gluing himself to the M6.
He was tired of explaining it and pretending he'd
moved on. He really hadn't. Soon enough it would
be a badge of honour, not something to be excused.*

*He stretched and opened his eyes. The sun had
already risen – of course it had, it was summer. He
reached reflexively for his phone and checked himself. Use your watch now. Max got up quietly and
went out on the deck, trying not to disturb the men
dozing around him. Most of them worked on the
windfarms, four weeks on, two weeks off.*

*It was time to do it. He took his phone out of his
pocket. There was no signal out here on the North
Sea, which helped. It also helped that he didn't need
the videos and photos that kept the Shetland part of
him alive in Manchester. Also, she was on the island,
and either it would work out or it wouldn't, in which*

case he didn't want to have anything to remember her by. Numbers and passwords were written down in three places and stowed in different parts of his backpack. He hoped he could burn them after a couple of years.

His story would be very simple. He'd lost his phone. He just wouldn't get another one. He'd work, he'd think, he'd read, his mind would be clear. If someone asked him for his number he'd say, If you want me again look for me under your boot-soles, *like Walt Whitman.*

OK. He threw the phone over the rail, and turned away.

▸ ▸ ▸ ▸ ▸ ▸

Anecdotally, Edward Ludlam was an eighteenth-century weaver from Leicestershire, who smashed two knitting frames after either being whipped for idleness or admonished by his father. When a group of textile workers began to smash up factory equipment that they feared would make their skills obsolete, they signed their letters and proclamations 'Ned Ludd', and became known as Luddites. In 1812 – despite a passionate intervention by Lord Byron on behalf of the frame-breakers – the government made smashing frames punishable by death. This, along with the threat of penal transport to Australia, put an end to the movement. 'Luddite' became an insult. But nostalgia for what the Luddites had wanted to achieve – the prizing of craftsmanship over technology – did not go away. While the original movement tried to defend craftsmen's livelihoods against mechanisation, its successors were more concerned about the effect of technology on wider society.

That concern crystallised in 1996 at the Second Luddite Congress in Ohio, an account of which appeared in a Quaker journal in the same year. There was no mention of the internet in its tentative manifesto. Email and websites were still emerging from the universities where they began. And as Quakers, the speakers were opposed to any form of violence. But many of the suggestions about how they should live would be familiar to a *Guardian* reader in the early 2020s.

> *We can slow the traffic in our neighbourhoods . . . We can eat locally grown food . . . We can drive less or not at all . . . libraries are some of the few places left in society where we truly share . . . We can take the interests, concerns, and imagination of children as a guideline.*[44]

Of course, I am not suggesting that everyone who shares these aspirations has Luddite tendencies. In fact, owning a mobile phone makes some of them easier. But when they rejected mainstream media and globalisation and wanted to slow the pace of change and fully understand the things around them, the Second Luddites were coming up with ideas that would achieve mainstream popularity twenty-five years later.

The Second Luddites' preoccupation with childhood is significant. It, too, has roots in the industrial revolution. In William Blake's *Songs of Innocence and Experience*, freedom and play are cruelly taken away by work before children have the chance to enjoy them. The chimney sweeps in his poems naively trust that their suffering will be rewarded in heaven, but Blake tells us it is not so.

For this movement, institutional trust was risky. Many of the Second Luddites favoured homeschooling for their children, and home births. Interpersonal trust, understood as community, would replace dependency on machines. Things that were too difficult for non-specialists to understand were regarded with suspicion, and community sufficiency was the ideal. One farmer spoke of how he didn't 'make money – just a living' because he wanted to be free from 'the money economy'.

Some of this thinking was shared by Ted Kaczynski, better known as the Unabomber. Kaczynski believed that the industrial revolution and subsequent technologies were destroying nature and had led to the destruction of small communities. Until his brother reported him to the FBI, he sent bombs by mail to people involved with modern technology and published his manifesto in exchange for a promise to give up violence. Naturally, the Second Luddites firmly rejected Kaczynski (while wondering whether he would have turned to violence had he felt part of a community), and most strands of neo-Luddism prefer to distance themselves from mainstream society rather than trying to destroy the technology that drives it.

⊳ ⊳ ⊳ ▶ ▶ ▶

But what will happen when it becomes more and more difficult to live without that technology? This is one of the scenarios imagined by the College of Policing when it thought about how the police might operate in 2040.[45] By the late 2020s, its report predicted, 'practical opportunities for maintaining privacy [might become] almost impossible' and among a minority who opposed the tech hegemony, collective resistance might grow. In this scenario, a 'neo-Luddite' group attacked AI labs.

It's very plausible. Anti-technology feeling spilled over during the COVID pandemic when the notion that 5G was spreading coronavirus led to dozens of arson attacks on phone masts. Later, anti-vaxxers attacked testing centres. These outbreaks of violence were linked to the 'plandemic' movement and fears about biosurveillance, including objections to vaccine passports. Anti-vaxxers argued that 'natural immunity' was better than the immunity that jabs gave them. They sought ways to make their bodies healthier and better able to fight off infection. These strategies had been developing for many years, as parents resisted the giving of vaccines to their children. Extending the same principles to COVID jabs involved no great leap of imagination. For some people who felt oppressed by lockdowns and mask mandates, rejecting jabs also offered a feeling of control and autonomy that the pandemic had taken away.

The experience of COVID suggests that violent opposition to AI could emerge if the research that's being undertaken seems to present a clear threat to civil liberties and – most importantly – the freedom of the individual. This could be problematic for researchers and governments who are experimenting with AI, especially if it's to be used for surveillance purposes. On the one hand, if they want to build trust among a frequently sceptical population, they need to be frank and transparent about what they are trying to do. But, on the other, their instincts may be to play down the possible uses of their research for fear of stoking opposition.

All this is complicated further by the sheer difficulty of explaining how AI works in simple terms. It makes the workings of the European Parliament look like a picture book. 'For regulatory purposes ... the logic or intent behind the output of systems can often be extremely hard to explain,' says a government policy paper on regulating AI.[46] The risks of AI are so hard to predict that rather than drawing up a list of what they might be, the government wants to look at them on a case-by-case basis, for fear of stifling innovation. Still, one of the guiding principles will be to:

> *Make sure that AI is appropriately transparent and explainable ... Presently, the logic and decision making in AI systems cannot always be meaningfully explained in an intelligible way, although in most settings this poses no substantial risk.*

In some high-risk cases, where the AI decision-making might be challenged in court, it anticipates that a system might be banned if the decisions it is making 'cannot be explained'.

It isn't hard to imagine why a neo-Luddite group might object to this reasoning. Research may be carried out that will be too complex to be challenged in court. Who decides whether it is too complex to be explained? Who can realistically challenge a decision like that? Won't the sophistication and usefulness of the algorithm be touted as a reason to proceed with it, outweighing the worries about whether a lay person can understand it? Is transparency even possible under these circumstances?

Most people won't be overly troubled by such questions. We routinely trust and benefit from technology that most of us can't explain – planes, cars, the internet itself. But the scope of the decisions that AI will make about our relationship with the state puts them in a different category. They are not just spatial and mechanical: they will decide how, and by how much, the state will help us.

AI is already used to assess benefit claims. Given the scale of the pressure on the National Health Service, it will be tempting to use it to adjust waiting lists, promoting some and deprioritising others. In any situation where people are competing for a scarce resource – council or social housing, expensive treatments, disability payments – AI has the potential to play a role. And the people who will be most affected by these decisions, with a few exceptions, are unlikely to be able to challenge them. Will they really be able to raise the funds to hire a barrister for a judicial review of their position on the council's waiting list? How many staff at the Department of Work and Pensions will be able to explain why the algorithm has down-graded a Personal Independence Payment claim? To most Britons, the administration of the welfare state is already a closed book. When the book is rewritten in a language that only a few specialists can understand, trust will break down further, and a sense of injustice and alienation is likely to grow.

Those who can afford to live independently of the state may be tempted to join communities of like-minded people, beyond the surveillance networks of cities. Indeed, this is already happening. In 2021, a community of largely German-speaking 'free think-ers' settled in a remote part of Paraguay, united by the belief that COVID was 'just a flu' and that masks cut people off from each other. They called their land El Paraíso Verde ('Green Paradise').[47] El Paraíso's Instagram account portrays a bucolic paradise of butterflies, hand-ploughing, and communal meals. The health centre specialises in 'naturopathy'.

The fundamental principles of El Paraíso Verde rely overwhelmingly on interpersonal trust. 'Every individual sets an example of honesty, sincerity and trustworthiness,' say the founders. The residents try whenever possible to keep their agreements verbal, though some have to be written down to avoid misunderstandings.

Paradise is not untroubled. Some settlers have been thrown out. There are disputes with other local landowners. Nonetheless, in its desire to live as far as possible beyond the reach of law, the community is a particular manifestation of distrust for institutions and unaccountable decision-making.

Things will be different for those who cannot afford to buy land or emigrate. Some, like our hypothetical friend Max, may choose a life that as far as possible eschews digital technology. Others might decide to express their frustration with violence. What unites them is a desire for the revival of interpersonal trust and a rejection of systems and technologies they do not understand. They will not take the digitised state on trust.

Neom

All men live in full view, so that all are obliged both to perform their ordinary task and to employ themselves well in their spare hours.

– Thomas More, Utopia

As we've seen, in the past couple of decades people have been quite willing to exchange their data for personalised services and the ability to do things quickly and easily. The pandemic accelerated that trend, as COVID created the desire to feel 'safe' among other vaccinated people. But what if, by handing over your data, you could gain access to a different society altogether – one which emerged from another culture, and was designed to offer a refuge from the pollution and crime of the rest of the world?

This city of nine million people would constantly monitor your health so that diseases were spotted early and treated quickly. Even though it was built in the desert, it would have an optimal amount of sunlight and shade. The air would be filtered. No one would drive a car, so there would be no traffic accidents. What if, somewhere thousands of miles away, people begin dying of a mysterious respiratory disease in a crowded city? This haven would be the first to close its borders.

This is the promise of Neom's The Line, a 170 kilometre long, 200 metre wide 'linear city' currently being built in Saudi Arabia by the Saudi prince Mohammed bin Salman (MBS – the M of Neom comes from his name). And the price of this Elysium is your data, which Neom will pay you for. 'Without trust, there is no data,' said the CEO of Neom Tech, Joseph Bradley, in 2022. 'Without data, there is no value.' He is responsible for setting up a system that 'enables users to review and easily understand the intention behind the use of their personal data, while offering financial rewards for authorising the use of their data'.[48] What might that be like?

◂ ▸ ▸ ▸ ▸ ▸

Sara opened her laptop and joined a Zoom call. It was hosted by a woman in her late twenties with a New Zealand accent. 'I know you'll have lots of questions about The Line,' she said, 'and I'm here to answer them. But first I'd like to share a video of the new apartment complex we've just finished building in the Bellevue district, because it really is spectacular.'

The camera swept over a park. Japanese acers were growing alongside a stream, and a family were eating ice creams in the shade of a sequoia. Fifty metres up, a woman leant over a balcony. Through a vast window was a conservatory, and beyond that a rain shower in a wet room. A doorbell rang in the apartment. Standing outside was a crate on wheels. The woman opened it, took out a pizza box, and clicked the lid shut. A man inside the apartment spoke and one of the walls lit up to show three children waving.

'Family aren't really far away in The Line,' said the voiceover. 'You're connected to the whole world.'

Sara typed a question into the chat box.

'Someone's asked about doctors' appointments,' said the host. 'I guess you live in England, right? Well, let me reassure you. We don't expect that you'll need to see a physician urgently very often, because your Neom watch will pick up any problems very early, but if you do then a 24/7 on-call doctor is part of the package. You pay a small fee each time, but it's waived if you have fewer than three callouts a year.'

My God, Sara thought. Just imagine. No more pleading with the receptionist to see the GP. Never having to endure A&E again. Why couldn't Britain be like this?

▶ ▶ ▶ ▶ ▶ ▶

Neom's marketing rarely acknowledges exactly where it is or the jurisdiction in which it sits. Countries like the UK sell themselves as good places to do business because of the certainty implied by their legal traditions. London law firms and barristers earn billions from this reputation and the trust it embodies. But in Saudi Arabia, as Amnesty put it in 2021:

> *The crackdown continued on the rights to freedom of expression, association and assembly. The Specialised Criminal Court handed down heavy prison terms to individuals for their human rights work and expression of dissenting views.*

Amnesty has described Saudi trials as 'grossly unfair'. According to them, this is not a country where locals, let alone foreigners, can expect a fair trial or proper legal representation. Sex outside marriage (and only heterosexual marriage is recognised) is a crime, and the maximum sentence is the death penalty. Criticising the regime is not tolerated: in August 2022 Salma al-Shebab, a Saudi dental student who was studying in Leeds, was sentenced to thirty-four years in prison for posting tweets that the Specialised Criminal Court considered to have undermined public order. She has two young children.[49]

Al-Shebab is thought to have been charged after she was reported on the Saudi government's Kollona Amn (We Are All Security) app, which citizens can download to their phones and use to report allegedly criminal activity. In the same month as al-Shebab was jailed, Neom launched an advertising campaign featuring a woman in Western dress running out of a grey, dismal urban landscape into The Line, where she flies through the city, skimming over pools of water and alongside tree-lined balconies. It ran extensively on Twitter ¶

There is much that we don't know about Neom, including how it will be governed and the laws it will impose on residents. Neom is trying to attract

---

¶ Incidentally, the Saudi connection with Twitter doesn't end there. Four per cent of the platform is owned by Prince Alwaleed, a cousin of MBS, though their relationship has not always been healthy: MBS and his uncle locked him up in the Ritz-Carlton hotel in Riyadh in 2017 and only let him go after he paid an undisclosed sum to the government, as detailed here: https://www.theguardian.com/world/2020/nov/19/saudi-accounts-emerge-of-ritz-carlton-night-of-the-beating residents from outside the Middle East, so it probably will not impose full Saudi law. People who live in Saudi Arabia's dedicated compounds for high-earning western workers are exempt from some laws, so those in The Line probably will be too. Living in The Line, as Bradley made clear, will involve handing over personal data about your movements to the city authorities. (Note that this information will be 'safe and protected'.) In return, you will have the privilege of living in a futuristic, climate-controlled space where the usual inconveniences of a city – pollution, crime, dirt, long commutes, bad neighbours, reminders of other people's poverty – will be absent. AI will be constantly deployed to make your life easier. The executive director explains:

> If the cognitive system can see that every morning at 8.15am, there are a large amount of people that want the lift on the 50th floor to go to the 60th floor then you are able to make the lives of those people easier by ensuring the elevator is waiting there for them.[50]

Currently absent from Neom's vision is any ability for individuals to say whom they want to represent them, or lobby for changes to the way The Line is governed. Your relationship with Neom will presumably be based on a contract in which you agree to hand over data and follow The Line's rules. Once that's signed, you have entered into a contractual relationship. That may be a reasonable trade, depending on your outlook. It's certainly a better deal than the one an authoritarian regime typically offers its people. But it is not democratic.

Scholars of democracy have pointed out how elected leaders – Donald Trump is the obvious example – can undermine the system that put them in power.[51] They gradually capture these institutions by packing them with cronies, starving opponents of funds, and passing laws that favour their own interests. By running down public services, they encourage people to lose trust in the ability of government to change their lives for the better.

But while all these things undermine people's faith that democracy can create a society they want to live in, and make them more likely to turn to authoritarian government at home, the existence of a place like The Line is another kind of threat to the existence of liberal democracies. Why sit around while institutions crumble? Why endure the disintegration of the society you used to know? Thousands of miles away is a cleaner, healthier, more beautiful alternative ready to welcome you. The Puritans made a similar calculation in the seventeenth century.

The Line's new citizens will have a multitude of reasons for moving to the Saudi enclave. Some knowledge work can be done from anywhere. Parts of the US and southern Europe are increasingly inhospitable in summer due to the climate emergency. They may be willing to give up patient confidentiality in exchange for prompt medical treatment. Perhaps they simply do not trust western governments to tackle their problems. They may see worries about privacy and open justice as luxuries, which were absent or eroded in the countries they have come from.

And Saudi Arabia is likely to point out that Neom's use of data is, at least in theory, more transparent than the tracking that we have come to accept as the price of platform services like Google Maps. Nominally, we consent to it, but how many of us understand the uses to which it is being put? Neom, on the other hand, says it will give future residents the ability to review what it uses their data for. Instead of the messy and constantly changing relationship between people and an elected government, in which people fight for the state's dwindling resources and gradually lose faith in its ability to provide them, The Line's citizens will, MBS hopes, feel part of an endeavour in which everyone gives up some of their privacy in the service of a better and healthier life.

So what will happen to someone who breaks the rules? We can only guess at that, given that The Line does not yet exist and Saudi Arabia has not yet addressed the question. But the Neom authorities will have an advantage over the governments of conventional states, who have to lock up, fine or otherwise punish an offender. They can simply expel a Line resident for breach of contract – in the same way that a social media site can ban an individual. Policing an AI-led state might turn out to be surprisingly similar to removing an avatar from the metaverse, even if the consequences for the individual are rather more frightening.

Deepfakes, the Media and the BBC

I have to be seen to be believed
— Queen Elizabeth II, reportedly[52]

Even when you have lost nothing because of it, the feeling that you have been deceived is unpleasant. It leaves most people feeling vulnerable and ashamed. (Believe me: while I was writing this book, I lost thousands of pounds to an online fraud. I told only three friends about it, even after I got the money back.) In France, the expression *se faire rouler dans la farine* (to get yourself rolled in flour) means that you've been swindled. Everyone can see it, and you look ridiculous afterwards. You were just too trusting. Even on April Fools' Day, when thousands of others will have fallen for the same thing, realising that you're among those who have been fooled is discombobulating.

As humans, we like storytelling, and we like listening to other people's stories. We are accustomed to the idea that fiction can express some ideas more compellingly than grubby, confusing reality does. (The real Julius Caesar was probably less interesting than Shakespeare's character, just as *The Crown* strives to make the royals more compelling than they likely are.) The most successful deepfakes will exploit this to the full. They will exist on a knife-edge between credibility and fantasy: believable enough to be credible, startling enough to transcend mundane reality. Those who are fooled by them will have every reason to want to believe that their credulity was justified.

> ▶ ▶ ▶ ▶ ▶ ▶

Elizabeth II died on 8 September 2022. A few days after she passed away peacefully at Balmoral Castle, a video emerged that shook the public's faith in the British monarchy.

The Queen looked frail. She was wearing a pale blue dress and sitting next to a window that appeared to look out over her Sandringham estate. 'I am ninety-five years old,' she said. 'In normal circumstances, I would look forward to speaking to you in my Christmas message. Yet I have asked one of the people whom I most trust to record this message. It will be released soon after I have gone.'

She paused. 'In many ways, this has been a painful decision. You will all know how highly I value the royal succession and the sacrifices that it demands. I deeply regret that my grandson Harry felt unable to continue with his duties. But it is on an even more important matter that I speak to you today.

'It is a decision that grieves me greatly.

'My eldest son has waited patiently for many years to become King. However, I must ask my government to withhold the Crown from Charles, and to pass it directly to my grandson William.

'I do not consider that Charles is able to fulfil the great demands and burdens to which kingship will subject him.

'I hope and trust that William, when he becomes King, with the help and support of his wife Catherine, will bear the responsibility and duties of his role as wholeheartedly as I have tried to do.'

The Queen smiled gently, and the video ended.

Within a few hours, the YouTube footage had been watched millions of times all over the world. Crowds began to gather outside Clarence House, where Charles was grieving for his mother. A walk-about to inspect the flowers left in Green Park was cancelled. William was glimpsed at the wheel of a Land Rover in Norfolk, ashen faced.

The following day, the clamour for an explanation grew. 'MY SON, MY SON' *splashed the* Daily Mail. *The* Sun *was forthright:* 'SHE WANTED WILLS – AND WE DO TOO'.

Two days later, the Palace put out an unusually long press release. 'The Royal Family is dismayed to note that a "deepfake" video of the late Queen Elizabeth has been widely circulated on the internet,' *it read.* 'This video was generated from the thousands of images of the Queen, and the many recordings of her voice, that are available online.*

'It has no basis in reality. The Queen, and the rest of the Royal Family, were united in their intention that her eldest son should succeed her.'

Numerous columnists argued that such a thing could only have happened thanks to the appalling influence of the Netflix series The Crown *on the public imagination, which had blurred the link between reality and fiction. The editor of the* Sun *resigned. The coronation of King Charles III went ahead as planned. Yet for many supporters of the monarchy, even though they could not be sure of its authenticity, the video seemed to express reasonable questions about the Queen's opinion of Charles. It might not be real, but it was definitely the kind of thing she would have felt, and probably thought*

about doing. Affection for the late queen grew.
Doubts about the new king resurfaced.

Deepfakes will take advantage of our instinct to trust
others, and our reluctance to accept that we've been
hoodwinked. They will tell stories that are more
compelling than real life and fit seamlessly into narratives that are already emerging. Thanks to the ease
with which video and photos can now be shared,
doctored images can spread extremely quickly
through WhatsApp[53], even without the endorsement
of any media outlet. And they will make the job of
investigative journalists and reporters considerably
more difficult.

In the past, when a source passed documents,
footage or a recording to a journalist, the reporter
usually found it easy to identify whether they were
genuine. There were exceptions — in 1983 a forger
fooled several outlets into publishing 'Hitler's
diaries', and the infamous 1934 photo of the 'Loch
Ness monster' hung around for decades before being
debunked — but video and audio has been much
harder to fake. This will change as deepfakes become
more convincing. Reporters will have to rely much
more on the credibility of their sources, and sources

will have to place even more trust in journalists to protect them in the face of widespread scepticism and demands for proof. Those media outlets that do fall for fakes are likely to suffer a serious loss of public trust.

Of course, the BBC and other organisations that carry out fact-checking will probably soon rise to the challenge of identifying and exposing deepfakes. So let's recall some of the things senior politicians and journalists have said about the BBC. Nadine Dorries, the former culture secretary, described it as a 'polar bear on a shrinking ice cap'. The BBC 'have a world view and a view of the UK, which is, I think, sometimes very wrong,' she said. The former PM Liz Truss agreed, telling rival GB News that 'it's not the BBC, you know, you actually get your facts right.'[54]

From the other side of the political spectrum, in 2014 the *Guardian* columnist Owen Jones said the BBC was 'stacked full of right-wingers', the former BBC political editor Laura Kuenssberg was viciously attacked for her alleged bias against Labour, and Scottish nationalist campaigners regularly criticise it as a mouthpiece of the Westminster government. Hating on the BBC is a game that everyone can play.

As long as the criticism pours in from both the left and the right, the BBC might feel that, on balance, it is still basically impartial. Winston Churchill often complained about the corporation. But people who no longer trust the BBC now have hundreds of alternative English-language channels and sites where they can find their news, as well as the opportunity to curate their social feed to suit their views. So the BBC debunked that deepfake – *well, it would, wouldn't it? Basically she said what we all feel.* As far as these media are concerned, the BBC's existence is unwelcome competition and benefits from an unjustifiable public subsidy paid out of a licence fee that viewers might prefer to spend on them instead. They have every interest in running the corporation down. In turn, the BBC – trying to pre-empt criticism – adopts a nervous, defensive attitude, anxious to justify its own existence even as it worries about exceeding its remit. The strategy of undermining trust in the BBC is working. By 2022, 55 per cent of Britons said they trusted it, down from 75 per cent in 2018. Over a quarter said they *distrusted* it, up from 11 per cent.[55] This group is more likely to get most of their news from social media.

The solution can't be for the BBC to have to repeatedly try to prove its trustworthiness. Those efforts will inevitably fail if much of the rest of the media amplifies the people criticising it. First, it is important to break down the mutually enriching relationships between the BBC's rivals and the party in power. It should not, for example, be possible for an MP to earn money from hosting a regular chat show on a broadcaster or writing a weekly column – whether or not they use that forum to call for the abolition of the licence fee, as Jacob Rees-Mogg has done.[56] Next, the prime minister should no longer have the final say in who is appointed as chairman of the BBC.[57] The government should proactively endorse the BBC as a publicly funded service which is free to scrutinise and report on what it wishes, and make it clear that only in exceptional circumstances will it comment on the trustworthiness of the BBC's reporting. Lastly, the social media apps where increasing numbers of people get their news, such as YouTube and podcast apps, should actively promote publicly funded news channels. (This won't be easy: but when we ask people to fund media through taxes, we have a responsibility to bring it to the places where they spend their time, and not simply hope that they will go back to watching the ten o'clock news and turning on BBC radio.)

There is no going back to the pre-internet world, where people got most of their news from bulletins and paid-for papers. But there is an opportunity to stop actively undermining trust in the BBC and to remove the financial incentives for politicians to do so.

Police

Trust in the police is absolutely vital for a functioning society. According to Our World in Data, in most European countries people trust the police more than they trust each other,[58] and significantly more than they trust the political or legal systems. In Britain in particular, because of the tradition that 'the police are the public and the public are the police',[59] they attempt to bridge the gap between interpersonal and institutional trust. The concept of 'policing by consent' was first set out in 1829. It explains that the police can only keep the trust of the public if they 'secure and maintain' their respect:

> *To seek and preserve public favour, not by pandering to public opinion; but by constantly demonstrating*

absolutely impartial service to law ... by ready
offering of individual service and friendship to all
members of the public without regard to their wealth
or social standing, by ready exercise of courtesy and
friendly good humour; and by ready offering of
individual sacrifice in protecting and preserving life.[60]

As far as the public are concerned, the police are
struggling to live up to these values. Less than two-
thirds of people in London think the police treat
everyone fairly regardless of who they are, and
the figure is lower among ethnic minorities,[61] and
especially among black Londoners.[62] (In America,
revulsion at the murder of a black man, George
Floyd, by a white police officer has led to calls to
'defund the police'.[63]) Things are better in other parts
of Britain. Nearly nine in ten people say they trust
West Mercia police. Still, in 2022 public confidence
in their local police force had fallen to 68 per cent,
according to the annual Crime Survey.[64]

But as we saw earlier in this book, measuring trust
is not easy. It is a slippery, mutable concept that takes
on different meanings depending on the object of the
trust and the person doing the trusting. When people
say they trust the police, do they trust them because
they prevent crime? That might involve doing things

that are, to say the least, not 'friendly'. Or do they want to feel they can approach the police and get their help when they need it? Could we find a way to identify would-be police officers who are not trust-worthy? Given the murder of Sarah Everard by a Metropolitan Police officer in 2021, it's tempting.

› › › › › ›

He'd passed his driving test first time. Freddie had a BSc in criminology from the University of Manchester and had been a Young Leader in the Scouts. He'd known since he was ten that he wanted to be a policeman, and he wasn't about to settle for the West Mercia force or the British Transport Police when the Met was recruiting graduates.

Freddie had gone out on patrol with a couple of plain-clothes sergeants – that was part of the recruit-ment process – and was pretty sure he'd impressed them, though he was worried he came across as a bit idealistic and maybe even slightly naïve. He'd tried to hide it, though.

One hurdle remained: the subconscious preju-dices test, which the Met had introduced two years before. Undoubtedly, the force was in a better place than it had been in the mid-2020s, when officers rou-tinely shared racist WhatsApp memes, strip-searched teenage girls when their schools suspected them of smoking cannabis, and (at one station) were running a profitable drug-delivery business with substances confiscated from punters, all of whom had been let off 'this time'.

Known as SubPrej, the test didn't involve answering questions. In fact it demanded nothing of the would-be police recruits at all. Freddie synced his smartwatch to a Met app, sat in a small windowless room with high-definition CCTV cameras in each corner, and watched half an hour of footage. It was all genuine material that had been captured from the body-mounted cameras the police had started wearing in the late 2010s. People – some white, some not, all causing trouble in some way or another – loomed in and out of shot.

Freddie knew the app was measuring his pulse and his blood pressure. The cameras were also watching his face and eyes, looking for signs of – what? Frustration? Anger? Impatience? He tried to keep a poker face. The face he'd wear if he was being yelled at by a drunk bloke who looked like he might be about to pull a knife. Jesus, but this was depressing. Enough to make you ask for a transfer to cybercrime.

After twenty effortful minutes, it was all over. Freddie adjusted his watch. He'd hear in a couple of *days – it didn't take long for the AI to analyse the data and footage.*

▹ ▹ ▸ ▸ ▶ ▶

Fictional Freddie is probably about five at the time of writing this book, and in one of its future scenarios, the College of Policing suggests that police vetting could include testing of subconscious prejudices by the year 2037.[65] In this story I've speculated about the parameters of the 'SubPrej' test, bearing in mind that numerous AI programs already claim to interpret facial expressions and give some insight into the emotions they reveal.

Because of our appetite for fictional crime, our understanding of how the police behave and what they can do is partly rooted in drama. In crime series, thrillers and detective stories, people have learnt to seek closure. The idea that a perpetrator is still at large is unsettling. It makes you trust the people around you a little less. Viewers who see the angst a fictional detective is experiencing as they grapple with a case are likely to feel warmer towards a real member of the CID. And when that detective solves the problem with a combination of sleuthing, intuition and psychological insight, the satisfaction is immense. This flawed but trustworthy character has put things right through brains and force of will. The motive and the ingenious method are laid bare.

In the future, as AI takes over more policing tasks – first the mundane ones, such as matching CCTV footage with pictures of suspects through facial recognition, then the task of trawling databases for incriminating patterns of behaviour – this charismatic detective will have less and less to do. Most crime is pretty dull, and the type that is growing fastest, online fraud, offers least excitement of all. Maverick fictional DSIs will no doubt develop a specialism in outwitting attempts by senior management to replace them with AI, just as Tom Cruise triumphantly insisted on the superiority of human pilots in *Top Gun: Maverick*. But it will become steadily more difficult for laypeople to understand how most crimes have been committed, let alone how it was solved, because the processes involved will be opaque. The College of Policing has warned that the police will need to recruit people with unusual intellectual and psychological qualities in order to solve cybercrime.

The effect on trust may well be corrosive – unless the police can persuade people that AI-led decisions can still be taken in a moral and ethical way. That is one of the reasons why future recruits like Freddie will be vetted so carefully. His judgment is valuable.

And as Britain becomes more diverse and mistrustful of institutions, a police force that doesn't do all it can to identify prejudiced applicants will lose the co-operation of the public.

Freddie will increasingly depend on AI to do his job. But as it takes over more tasks, and the public demand evidence that the police can still act independently and judiciously, his character will be more important than ever. Will AI be better at identifying his subconscious prejudices than the traditional recruitment processes? And what would it mean for Freddie, who has wanted to join the police for years, if he is rejected because of prejudices of which he was unaware?

If we aren't careful, we could find ourselves in a situation where AI is mistrusted by the public because its workings are mysterious, and probably subject to algorithmic bias – but still trusted enough to decide who should become a police officer in the first place. The way the police work will become increasingly hard to understand, even as statistics about their performance proliferate. At the same time, the police will be on the front line of the coming tensions over land. As property ownership becomes increasingly limited to those who inherit money and assets from their parents,[66] and people guard natural resources and fuel ever more jealously, the police will be called upon to defend the existing order. The job of 'offering . . . service and friendship to all members of the public without regard to their wealth or social standing' is about to get even more difficult.

Germany, where there have been repeated clashes between green activists trying to protect an area of ancient forest and the police charged with removing them,[67] is likely to be a harbinger of the dilemmas the police face as they try to enforce bitterly contested court rulings over who owns land and who has the right to exploit it. That brings us to another enormous test of our relationship with institutions and each other: the climate emergency.

Climate

We have not had long to enjoy our conquest of the world. It is less than four thousand years since Babylonians wrote the Code of Hammurabi, which protected farmers from the risk that a flood or drought would stop them being able to repay a loan.[68] Now we face the probability that substantial parts of the Earth will become uninhabitable, thanks to our efforts to make our lives more comfortable and pleasurable.

The threat of apocalypse is not new. Weather gods held terrifying power in most early cultures and people would sacrifice each other and their animals to appease them. Indeed, it was the ability to stave off cold, drought and floods that enabled complex civilisations to emerge. That is why the climate emergency poses a special threat to institutional trust – to things like insurance, property, and the certainty that you will always be able to live in the country where you were born. Likewise, it will break down movement and trade, encouraging countries that are relatively unaffected by global heating to close their borders, just as they did during the pandemic. Around 46,000 people crossed the Channel in small boats in 2022. It was enough for the government to pass a law that promised to deport them to Rwanda.

The people living in this new world will be much less likely to take risks. They will travel less, unless forced to do so because the places they lived in have become effectively uninhabitable. They will lose patience with institutions that have failed to protect them and their property. They will hold the European countries that industrialised first accountable for the damage carbon emissions have done, perhaps seeking reparations in exchange for global co-operation, or trying to punish them in other ways. They may well become deeply attached to the parts of the natural world that remain, fearful that they will be destroyed by fire or the need for new homes for displaced people. In some places, on the other hand, interpersonal trust may flourish as people shrink their circles of trust and become more dependent on each other for basic needs.

▷ ▷ ▷ ▷ ▷ ▷

Damp, seeping through the skirting boards. Mildew creeping into any clothing left in a drawer for too long. The whiff of black mould coming from a corner of the bedroom. The water had poured into the flat during the Great Severn Flood two years ago and had never really gone away. They had hoped for a hot summer to dry things out but El Niño or La Niña, Ella could never remember which, had been in the wrong cycle and the scorching temperatures had been interrupted by drenching rain every couple of weeks.

She knew that it was ultimately her own fault that she'd bought a basement flat on a floodplain. What she didn't understand was why no one had warned her that it was so prone to flood, and why she'd been able to get a mortgage for a place that was now unsaleable. Even if it were demolished no one in their right mind would build anything else here. Ella wondered if by the end of the century it would be like the Welsh villages that had been flooded to make reservoirs, and her flat would be left to the fish, swimming in and out of the kitchen cupboards.

Her brother had a place on a hill in Wales. At some point she would have to decide whether to cut her losses and go and live with him. Now the

*country was independent, and governed by a Green–
Plaid Cymru coalition, it was more difficult to move
there: it had taken full advantage of its high land,
and Snowdonia and mid-Wales were popular with
people who could work remotely. And Scotland and
Wales had rejoined the European Union, which was
only too happy to pay them to join the EU resettle-
ment scheme for climate migrants.*

*Lincolnshire, Bristol and parts of Kent were now
effectively uninhabitable. Many councils with higher
ground had closed their schools, foodbanks and
emergency shelters to people who hadn't lived there
for at least five years.*

*In some parts of England, farmers had converted
a field into a campsite, rented out parcels of land and
provided a toilet block. It wasn't much of a way to
live but as the months became years people began
to hope that the courts would give them squatters'
rights after a decade, though there was no legal
precedent for that. Other people were sharing homes
in a scheme that had first been tried at the beginning
of the war in Ukraine. The host got a payment. After
the Kent Storm, a lot of Airbnbs on higher ground
had been requisitioned by the government. Plenty
of people had challenged it in the courts, but just
as when they were told to stay at home during the*

pandemic, they'd had to accept it. In fact, grumbling about it was regarded as unpatriotic. The government compared it to taking in evacuees during the Second World War, which shut a lot of people up.

The thing that Ella found most difficult to accept was that everyone had known this would happen. She had seen maps from the 1990s that predicted the sea level rise. Yet developers had still built houses on the floodplains because the land was cheap. It was cheap because they knew it would flood. She didn't blame people for still burning fuel and eating meat. Most of them were just trying to live. But she did blame the property companies and the government for deceiving her.

For decades the government had been pandering to the elderly, anyway – protecting their incomes and healthcare, no matter what the cost to everyone else. In her most cynical mood, Ella noted that people were pampered until the point at which they became incapable of voting any more, at which point they were either confined in a room until they died (for the better-off) or handed over to their family to deal with.

The best you could say was that spending billions of pounds on renovating old buildings, which used to be quite normal, had become unthinkable now. Even Parliament wasn't going to be rebuilt. MPs had

been about to move out of the crumbling Palace of
Westminster when it had burnt down during the
45-degree summer of 2030 – a wood-fired pizza
oven in Whitehall had set a building alight, and the
flames had raced towards Big Ben and consumed the
Commons chamber. No one had tried to reconvene
the Lords, and most of the country had barely
noticed that it no longer met in person. English MPs
talked on Zoom and in regional chambers, but it was
hard to get much sense of what they were doing. The
tax take had fallen as displaced people refused to
register where they were ('I don't have a proper roof
over my head, so why should I pay anything?') and
were paid under the table in local cryptocurrencies.

   She'd heard about a man calling himself Noah
who was offering food, board and wifi to anyone
under fifty who would help him build and fit out
a vast ship to float on the flooded Norfolk Broads.
Those who wanted to stay on board when the ship
was finished would have the right to a cabin. When
a storm was coming, resident meteorologists would
predict it weeks in advance and direct the ship to
safe waters. Ella didn't know whether to trust
'Noah'. Communes were not her thing and clearly
the guy was a bit delusional to compare himself to a
man from the Old Testament. The thing was, what

*came next? Would the ship just float around for
ever? What was the purpose of it, besides survival?
She worried about her parents, who were hosting a
family from King's Lynn. She didn't know whether
they would feel any obligation towards their hosts if
Ella went away. She just wanted to know if she could
trust them.*

       ❙ ❱ ❱ ❱ ❱ ❱

This is rather a frightening scenario – though far
from apocalyptic. Perhaps the international bodies
we have built up since the Second World War will
be strong enough to halt, if not reverse, global
heating: and perhaps new technology will enable
us to mitigate its worst effects. Humans are capable
of extraordinary sacrifice if they believe that the
continued existence of their culture depends on it –
though it is much harder for us to act on a threat
that is not immediately lethal, and where the enemy
cannot be simply destroyed.

But the work of making the Earth habitable
again, and helping the people who believed they
owned a place in it, will demand a colossal effort.
The backlash against English councils which are
trying to limit the use of cars hints at how difficult
it will be to do things that affect some people more

than others.[69] During the pandemic, it proved very divisive to impose lockdowns in one city but not its neighbours.[70]

Perhaps the most important lesson to take from the pandemic is that trust in the government is reciprocal: a leader who inspires confidence need not resort to harsh policing and complex laws to persuade people to do as they say. As we saw in both the US and the UK, people who do not trust their leaders will turn to others to guide them through a crisis – and they will certainly find those aspirants online.

Conclusion

Trust has an ineffable quality that resists most of our attempts to quantify it. It's not a sin and it's not always a virtue. It can be good. It can be blindly foolish. We throw it out half-jokingly to people we've never met before to try to put them at their ease. *It's OK, I trust you.* We use it about a brand of soap, and about God. We reproach people for failing to live up to it. *I trusted you.* Very rarely – in Britain, anyway – do we simply say, with complete sincerity: *I trust you.* It goes better unsaid.

In the last thousand years, humans have gradually expanded their circles of trust. At first, trusting relationships were interpersonal or with God. Then people began to trust institutions like governments, banks and hospitals. In the past 150 years they have come to trust brands, too. Now we are developing new ways to establish each other's credibility, driven by artificial intelligence. If we are, as some people think, living in an Age of Uncertainty – dominated by fear of the climate and disease and an overwhelmed welfare state – then these new ways of establishing trust hold promise. But they also have the potential to provoke division, exclusion and ultimately isolation.

For politicians and journalists, one of the most alarming developments of recent times is people's growing trust in business (61 per cent, according to the annual Edelman survey) compared with governments (52 per cent) and the media (50 per cent). Taken at face value, that means people are more likely to trust the ads that pay for the news *than they trust the news itself, or the government they elected*.

Partly, this is down to complexity. Businesses that sell a service and are clear about what they offer are more readily understood and trusted than a state that withholds things from some people and gives them to others, all in exchange for taxes people have no choice but to pay. It's even harder for an institution to maintain credibility if its purpose is not properly explained to the public – as happened with European institutions in the UK.

What this means is that business has been able to foster trust much more easily than governments can. In fact, the trust-based systems we use most often are no longer controlled by the state. Although the image of King Charles III has now appeared on stamps and coins, it is more of a curiosity than part of everyday life. Most of us now use apps and email to communicate, and cards and phones to pay.

That's no bad thing. The future that Margaret Atwood wrote about in *The Handmaid's Tale*, where women's bank accounts were abruptly frozen by the government, is less likely to come true. Few of us want business to do the bidding of the state, as it does in China. But as we are discovering, giving Big Tech responsibility for making the rules on freedom of speech isn't very satisfactory either. Nor are tech companies very good at recognising when their products harm people, or what they could do about it without breaking their business model.

Powerful though it is now, the trust we have in business may prove to be surprisingly thin. When catastrophes happen, as when COVID struck in the spring of 2020, some businesses will quickly adapt to the new reality. But people will again turn to government to help them cope and know how to behave. Only then will we see whether institutional trust can hold up under extreme pressure.

꙳ ꙳ ꙳ ꙳ ꙳ ꙳

People *want* to trust their neighbours and the institutions they rely on. We know this because those who have lost confidence in some aspect of government generally seek out a new community which they feel shares their values – whether in the real world or through social media and, potentially, the metaverse. And artificial intelligence makes it easier than ever for them to do that. It offers the choices and autonomy that government does not. What chance does the democratic social contract have when so many more attractive contracts are available? As Saudi Arabia has realised, governments that deploy artificial intelligence cleverly do not necessarily alienate people: in fact, they may prove to be rather attractive. One woman's dystopia is another's safe and properly policed refuge.

But perhaps the most frightening future for artificial intelligence – and one which has been very little dis-cussed – is the enormous temptation to use AI to make decisions we do not want to take full responsibility for. We may tell ourselves that we're only delegating these decisions because AI makes them faster or better than we do. Why send in a soldier when a robot will do the same job? But in truth, in the case of killer weaponry like drones, we're doing it to avoid the ethical and moral trade-offs that would otherwise have made us think twice about acting at all. How can we make finely balanced judgments about whether to kill an enemy when we feel protected from the moral and physical consequences of our actions?

One solution, argues the military technology specialist Sorin Adam Matei, might be to program killer robots with a sense of their own vulnerability.[71] It's an elegant idea, but not one that will appeal to military commanders. And it relies on whether we can trust AI programmers to be able to simulate vulnerability. We'd also have to trust our opponents to play by the rules and not try to hack our killer robots and make them switch sides. In wartime, fair play goes out of the window.

The institutions that do manage to win public trust will be those that are frank about what they are trying to do with AI and how they will stop it from perpetuating – even worsening – the inequalities in democratic societies. Most importantly, they won't use it as a cop-out to avoid taking personal responsibility for decisions that are unpleasant or complex.

Sometimes we would like to equate trust with perfect transparency. But as technology and AI become more complex, full transparency places an intolerable cognitive burden on us. It's as if an air-line could reassure its passengers by sending them the details of pre-flight checks. Trust *demands* a leap of faith – a leap that can only be made when the actions someone takes bear out the trust we want to place in them, and the repercussions of letting us down are severe.

But perhaps the most urgent thing governments should understand is that insecurity and fear breed *distrust*. In Britain, the past decade has seen a steady erosion of people's confidence in the state. They no longer trust the NHS to treat them quickly enough, or the police to treat them fairly and respectfully. The law, as they see it, is administered in such a way as to favour the better-off. Meanwhile politicians, through the personal choices they make, have driven home the message that state-funded services are inadequate. Ministers have cut funding to schools even as they choose to privately educate their own children. They seek to undermine public confidence in the BBC, negotiate lucrative individual contracts with rival broadcasters, and call for the abolition of the licence fee.

This distrust has awful consequences. Those who can afford it hoard property, afraid that the state won't pay for their needs when they are sick or old. Giving to charity becomes too risky: what if that money is desperately needed later? Chip away at the social contract and the basic expectation that the state will protect you from catastrophe, and people react fearfully. That was dimly understood during the pandemic, when older people were particularly vulnerable. The insight is already slipping away.

And crucially, a state whose people no longer trust it will not necessarily undergo radical or revolutionary change. The better-off may emigrate to places where they feel safer, or make themselves as independent from the state as they possibly can. They may give up on institutional trust, and instead try to revive societies based on interpersonal trust. They may establish walled-off communities online where they can find emotional or intellectual solace. For as long as they are healthy and can meet their physical needs, this may feel like enough.

It is not necessarily too late to build up trust again. Most of us are still at the *I trusted you* stage of shock and disillusionment – still willing to be convinced that government could act to address the uncertainty we feel. The desire to place our trust in something that would deserve it will not go away. If this society fails to provide it, other states and virtual worlds will take the place of ours.

Endnotes

Foreword

1. '*Guardian* judged to be most trustworthy newspaper' (20 January 2005), https://www.the guardian.com/media/2005/jan/20/theguardian. pressandpublishing; '*The Guardian* is most trusted by its readers' (13 August 2020), https:// www.theguardian.com/media/2020/aug/13/ the-guardian-is-most-trusted-by-its-readers-among-uk-newspapers-finds-ofcom

2. Edelman Trust Barometer 2023, https://www. edelman.com/trust/2023/trust-barometer

3. '*Truthiness* voted 2005 Word of the Year by American Dialect Society' (6 January 2006), https:// americandialect.org/Words_of_the_Year_2005.pdf

A Brief History of Trust

4. Psalm 146: 3–5, https://www.bible.com/bible/392/psa.146.3-5.CEV

5. Locke, John, *The Second Treatise on Civil Government* (1689), https://wwnorton.com/college/history/archive/resources/documents/ch04_03.htm

6. Metropolitan Police: facial recognition, https://www.met.police.uk/advice/advice-and-information/fr/facial-recognition

7. YouGov, 'By 51% to 42%, Londoners don't trust the Metropolitan Police' (2023), https://yougov.co.uk/topics/politics/articles-reports/2023/02/10/51-42-londoners-dont-trust-metropolitan-police

8. *Meet the Fockers* (Universal Pictures, 2004)

9. Putnam, R. D., *Bowling Alone: The Collapse and Revival of American Community* (Simon & Schuster, 2000)

10. EconPort: Trust Game, https://www.econport.org/econport/request?page=man_tfr_experiments_trustgame

11. Casino Royale (Columbia Pictures, 2006)

12. Commons Hansard, Helmsley, Viscount, *Parliamentary Franchise (Women) Bill,* (vol. 36), debated on Thursday 28 March 1912, https://hansard.parliament.uk//Commons/1912-03-28/debates/e3b37698-57e8-40a9-8c1d-ec80c7757d18/ParliamentaryFranchise(Women)Bill

13. Office for National Statistics, 'Trust in government, UK: 2022', https://www.ons.gov.uk/peoplepopulationandcommunity/wellbeing/bulletins/trustingovernmentuk/2022

14. Edelman, 2022 Edelman Trust Barometer, https://www.edelman.com/trust/2022-trust-barometer

15. Johnson, Boris, 'I cannot stress too much that Britain is part of Europe – and always will be', *Daily Telegraph* (26 June 2016), https://www.telegraph.co.uk/politics/2016/06/26/i-cannot-stress-too-much-that-britain-is-part-of-europe--and-alw/

The COVID-19 Pandemic

16. Office for National Statistics, 'Trust in government, UK: 2022', op cit.

17. UK Health Security Agency, 'COVID-19 confirmed deaths in England (to 31 January 2021): report, https://www.gov.uk/government/publications/covid-19-reported-sars-cov-2-deaths-in-england/covid-19-confirmed-deaths-in-england-report

18. Moore, Sian, Clamp, Christina, Amendah, Eklou R., Carter, Nigel, Burns, Calvin and Martin, Wesley, 'Why some health and social care workers resisted compulsory COVID-19 vaccination', LSE COVID-19 blog (18 May 2022), https://blogs.lse.ac.uk/covid19/2022/05/18/

why-some-health-and-social-care-workers-resisted-
compulsory-covid-vaccination/

19. Pfaff, Katharina, Neumayer, Eric and
Plümper, Thomas, 'Querdenken: the German
anti-lockdown movement that thrives on public
distrust', LSE COVID-19 blog (29 September
2021), https://blogs.lse.ac.uk/covid19/2021/09/29/
querdenken-the-german-anti-lockdown-movement-
that-thrives-on-public-distrust/

20. Fancourt, Daisy, Steptoe, Andrew, Wright
and Liam, 'The Cummings effect: politics,
trust and behaviours during the COVID-19
pandemic', *The Lancet* (6 August 2020), https://
www.thelancet.com/journals/lancet/article/
PIIS0140-6736(20)31690-1/fulltext

21. Besley, Tim and Dann, Chris, 'When
we talk about state capacity to deal with
COVID, we shouldn't ignore interpersonal
trust', LSE COVID-19 blog (5 January 2022),
https://blogs.lse.ac.uk/covid19/2022/01/05/
when-we-talk-about-state-capacity-to-deal-with-
covid-we-shouldnt-ignore-interpersonal-trust/

22. Montacute, Rebecca, Holt-White, Erica,
Anders, Jake, Cullinane, Carl, De Gennaro,
Alice, Early, Erin, Shao, Xin, and Yarde, James
(2022). 'Wave 1 Initial Findings – Education

Recovery and Catch Up'. COVID Social Mobility
and Opportunities study (COSMO) Briefing
No. 2. London: UCL Centre for Education
Policy and Equalising Opportunities and Sutton
Trust, https://cosmostudy.uk/publications/
education-recovery-and-catch-up
23. 'Why can't I get care? Older people's
experiences of care and support', Age UK (February
2023), https://www.ageuk.org.uk/globalassets/
age-uk/documents/campaigns/care-in-crisis/why-
cant-i-get-care-report.pdf

Law
24. BBC News: 'Theresa May under fire over
deportation cat claim' (4 October 2011), https://
www.bbc.co.uk/news/uk-politics-15160326
25. Remarks by President Trump at a roundtable
discussion on tax reform, White Sulphur Springs
Civic Center, West Virginia (5 April 2018), https://
trumpwhitehouse.archives.gov/briefings-statements/
remarks-president-trump-roundtable-discussion-
tax-reform/
26. Joint Committee on Human Rights: Every
Fixed Penalty Notice issued under coronavirus
regulations must be reviewed (27 April 2021),
https://committees.parliament.uk/committee/93/

human-rights-joint-committee/news/154842/
joint-committee-on-human-rights-every-fixed-
penalty-notice-issued-under-coronavirus-
regulations-must-be-reviewed/
27. Ministry of Justice: Courts data, tribunals,
https://data.justice.gov.uk/courts/tribunals
28. 'Kate Forbes says she'll defend abortion
rights depite personal beliefs', *The National*
(22 February 2023) https://www.thenational.scot/
news/23338379.kate-forbes-says-defend-abortion-
rights-despite-personal-beliefs/
29. Pew Research Center, 'Most Democrats
and Republicans know Biden is Catholic, but
they differ sharply about how religious he is'
(30 March 2021), https://www.pewresearch.
org/religion/2021/03/30/most-democrats-and-
republicans-know-biden-is-catholic-but-they-differ-
sharply-about-how-religious-he-is/

The Metaverse

30. McDonell, Stephen, 'China social media:
WeChat and the Surveillance State', BBC News
(7 June 2019), https://www.bbc.co.uk/news/
blogs-china-blog-48552907
31. Tesco GetGo, https://www.tesco.com/zones/
getgo

32. Sharma, Vivek, 'Introducing a Personal Boundary for Horizon Worlds and Venues', Meta (4 February 2022) https://about.fb.com/news/2022/02/personal-boundary-horizon/

33. Chalmers, David, *Reality+: Virtual Worlds and the Problems of Philosophy* (Allen Lane, 2022)

34. Clegg, Nick, 'Making the metaverse: What it is, how it will be built, and why it matters' (18 May 2022), https://nickclegg.medium.com/making-the-metaverse-what-it-is-how-it-will-be-built-and-why-it-matters-3710f7570b04

Artificial Intelligence

35. Asimov, Isaac, *Victory Unintentional* (1942)

36. *The Guardian*, 'Amazon agrees to buy Roomba maker iRobot for £1.7bn' (5 August 2022), https://www.theguardian.com/technology/2022/aug/05/amazon-buy-roomba-maker-irobot-vaccum

37. BBC News, 'David Cameron defends drone strike investigation' (12 January 2016), https://www.bbc.co.uk/news/uk-politics-35295400

38. Susskind, Jamie, *Future Politics: Living Together in a World Transformed by Tech* (2018)

39. Glover, Ellen, 'What is the Eliza effect?' (21 March 2023), https://builtin.com/artificial-intelligence/eliza-effect

40. Roose, Kevin, Twitter, 16 February 2023, https://twitter.com/kevinroose/status/1626216340955758594

41. Smith, Craig S., 'Hallucinations could blunt ChatGPT's success', IEEE Spectrum (13 March 2023), https://spectrum.ieee.org/ai-hallucination

42. Edelman Trust Barometer (2023), https://www.edelman.com/trust/2023/trust-barometer

Neo-Luddites

43. Menon, Anand, '2016: A review', UK in a Changing Europe (31 December 2016), https://ukandeu.ac.uk/2016-a-review/

44. Goodridge, Tom, *Friends Journal* (August 1996), https://www.friendsjournal.org/wp-content/uploads/emember/downloads/1996/HC12-50926.pdf

45. College of Policing, 'Policing in England and Wales: Future Operating Environment 2040' (2020), https://assets.college.police.uk/s3fs-public/2020-08/future-operating-environment-240.pdf

46. Policy paper: 'Establishing a pro-innovation approach to regulating AI', Gov.uk (updated 20 July 2022), https://www.gov.uk/government/publications/establishing-a-pro-innovation-approach-to-regulating-ai/establishing-a-pro-innovation-approach-to-regulating-ai-policy-statement

47. El Paraíso Verde Paraguay, https://paraiso-verde.com/en/el-paraiso-verde-in-the-heart-of-paraguay/

Neom
48. Farouk, Menna A., 'Saudi "surveillance city": Would you sell your data to The Line?, Reuters (23 August 2022), https://www.reuters.com/article/saudi-city-surveillance-idAFL8N2ZL0CM
49. *The Guardian*, 'Saudi woman given 34-year prison sentence for using Twitter' (16 August 2022), https://www.theguardian.com/world/2022/aug/16/saudi-woman-given-34-year-prison-sentence-for-using-twitter
50. Pendleton, Giles, 'Neom: The Line', https://www.neom.com/en-us/regions/theline
51. Tony Blair Institute for Global Change, 'The Populist Harm to Democracy: An Empirical Assessment' (26 December 2018), https://institute.global/policy/populist-harm-democracy-empirical-assessment

Deepfakes, the Media and the BBC
52. Quoted in Bedell Smith, Sally, *Elizabeth the Queen* (2012)
53. Rossini, Patricia, Mont'Alverne, Camila and Kalogeropoulos, Antonis (2023). Explaining beliefs

in electoral misinformation in the 2022 Brazilian election: The role of ideology, political trust, social media, and messaging apps. Harvard Kennedy School (HKS) Misinformation Review. https://doi.org/10.37016/mr-2020-115

54. Tobitt, Charlotte, 'Liz Truss versus the media: Her attacks on the BBC and "left-wing" questioning', Press Gazette (22 August 2022), https://pressgazette.co.uk/news/liz-truss-media-attacks-conservative-leadership/

55. Digital News Report 2022, Reuters Institute for the Study of Journalism, https://reutersinstitute.politics.ox.ac.uk/digital-news-report/2022/dnr-executive-summary

56. In January 2023 GB News announced that Jacob Rees-Mogg would host his own show on the channel. GB News, YouTube: 'Moggologue: We have no need for a state broadcaster', https://www.youtube.com/watch?v=7lvggJOb5-I

57. Brown, Faye, 'BBC chairman Richard Sharp confident he was "appointed on merit" after Boris Johnson loan row', Sky News, 24 January 2023, https://news.sky.com/story/bbc-chairman-richard-sharp-confident-he-was-appointed-on-merit-after-boris-johnson-loan-row-12794154

Police

58. Ortiz-Ospina, Esteban and Roser, Max, 'Trust', OurWorldInData.org (2016) https://ourworldindata.org/trust

59. Home Office, 'Definition of policing by consent' (10 December 2012), https://www.gov.uk/government/publications/policing-by-consent/definition-of-policing-by-consent

60. Ibid.

61. YouGov, 'By 51% to 42%, Londoners don't trust the Metropolitan Police' (2023), op. cit.

62. Evans, Amber, Olajide, Patrick and Clements, Jon, 'Crime, policing and stop and search: Black perspectives in context', Crest (8 November 2022), https://www.crestadvisory.com/post/report-stop-and-search-the-evidence

63. Lowrey, Annie, 'Defund the Police' *The Atlantic* (5 June 2020), https://www.theatlantic.com/ideas/archive/2020/06/defund-police/612682/

64. https://www.ons.gov.uk/peoplepopulationand community/crimeandjustice/bulletins/crimeinenglandandwales/yearendingseptember20 22#:~:text=2.-,Overall%20estimates%20of%20 crime,ending%20March%202020%20survey%20 data

65. College of Policing, 'Policing in England and Wales: Future Operating Environment 2040', op. cit.

66. Demos, 'A new age of inheritance: what does it mean for the UK?' (23 January 2023), https://demos.co.uk/project/a-new-age-of-inheritance-what-does-it-mean-for-the-uk/

67. See the Hambacher Forst Twitter account, https://twitter.com/HambiBleibt

Climate

68. The Code of Hammurabi, https://avalon.law.yale.edu/ancient/hamframe.asp

69. BBC News, 'Thousands join protest against traffic schemes' (18 February 2023), https://www.bbc.co.uk/news/uk-england-oxfordshire-64689171

70. Rigby, Beth, 'Coronavirus: Andy Burnham is the "King of the North" – a crown the PM believed he'd won', Sky News (21 October 2020)

Conclusion

71. Matei, Sorin, 'The first (and only) law of robotic warfare', The Strategy Bridge (17 November 2021), https://thestrategybridge.org/the-bridge/2021/11/17/the-first-and-only-law-of-roboticwarfare#:~:text=the%20law%20

of%20robotic%20warfare,losses%20in%20
a%20peer%20conflict.&text=Given%20
this%2C%20the%20law%20of,losses%20in%20
a%20peer%20conflict.

About the Series

Each volume in the FUTURES Series presents a vision imagined by an accomplished writer and subject expert. The series seeks to publish a diverse range of voices, covering as wide-ranging a view as possible of our potential prospects. Inspired by the brilliant 'To-Day and To-Morrow' books from a century ago, we ask our authors to write in a spirit of pragmatic hope, and with a commitment to map out potential future landscapes, highlighting both beauties and dangers. We hope the books in the FUTURES Series will inspire readers to imagine what might lie ahead, to figure out how they might like the future to look, and, indeed, to think about how we might get there.

Professor Max Saunders and Dr Lisa Gee
Series originators, University of Birmingham

The FUTURES Series was originally conceived by Professor Max Saunders and Dr Lisa Gee, both of whom work at the University of Birmingham. Saunders is Interdisciplinary Professor of Modern Literature and Culture and the author of *Imagined Futures: Writing, Science, and Modernity in the To-Day and To-Morrow* book series, 1923-31 (OUP 2019), and Gee is Assistant Professor in Creative Writing and Digital Media and Research Fellow in Future Thinking.

To find out more about their Future Thinking work visit www.birmingham.ac.uk/futures